T0064143

MY COMMITMENT
TO A
GREEN WORLD

MY COMMITMENT
——— TO A ———
GREEN WORLD

Sandhyavandanam

S. Venkatramanan

PARTRIDGE
A Penguin Random House Company

To order additional copies of this book, contact
Partridge India
000 800 10062 62
orders.india@partridgepublishing.com

www.partridgepublishing.com/india

Sandhyavandanam
is a practice done daily

♦

To Learn and Practice in our day-to-day
life to treat the abundance of Nature
at our doorstep with respect

♦

To train the Mind on how to live
Responsibly, Fearlessly and
Independently

♦

To get an OTP (one time password) to
refresh and reenergise oneself
instantaneously.

♦

To get Commited to Green World and
Welfare of Fellow men

♦

The following pages are written in the form of a direct dialogue - communication to a young reader and to those who would like to know the real significance of Sandhyavandanam. Suitable for group reading as well.

Acknowledgements

The principles and practices of a school of thought often gets shrouded in mechanical obscure procedures .This is true and applicable with a number of Hindu practices as well. Most of the Hindu practices were originally directed towards a happy and healthy living in the present world. But in practice this does not bring out that feeling. empty practices propelled me to revisit the Hindu thoughts all over again from the basics. The prevalent confusion and misinterpretation are to be acknowledged as the first source of inspiration to me for writing this book. In this process a number of people helped me with some fresh thoughts – linked direct or otherwise to understand the true values and original thoughts. My sincere thanks to all of them.

A candid introduction and exposure given during my early years, by my father Late Sri.K.Subramanian, has undoubtedly laid the foundation for my interest in this subject of the Hindu Practices. I respect and value his guidance and training in this regard.

My thanks to Sri. V. Balasubramaniam of Chinmaya nagar, Chennai for giving me an encouragement to write this book and Mr.Sundar Narayanaswami of **B**angalore for his candid comments to improve the book at its draft stage. My special thanks to Mr. Nilesh Joshi who took the photographs and the young Pranav for being the model for the photographs. I also record my thanks to my daughter Mrs. Atulya Bhardwaj for helping me on the cover page. I should thank my family for chipping in their view points at various stages. Mr. Sunil and Ms Jyoti Rani also helped me in preparing the Sanskrit portions of the manuscript. The Baraha team helped me in the finishing stages to get a good presentation.

I only sincerely hope that the book will trigger the thoughts of youngsters to see the intrinsic values of this practice of Sandhya vandhanam and not to do it mechanically as a ritual. Sandhyavandanam should be followed so as to develop a mind set to respect the nature and cosmic forces in and around us.

Partridge publishing came forward to assist me in publishing both the e-version and paper back. I must thank them for supporting this effort of mine.

S.Venkatramanan

PREFACE

There is a total unanimity among the Nations of the world to protect the Nature and to live in mutual dependence and coexistence with the various forms of Natural forces - water, fire, air, earth, space and the plant kingdom. Every international body wants this "mindset" to be the guiding factor in adopting and practicing any development plan - that uses one form of natural source or the other.

How to develop and sustain this mind set among the citizens and help them to adopt the principle in their day to day life? While this mindset can be instilled in a school or a college, to sustain the need is to remind this principle- every dawn and dusk. Such daily "Self reminders" will help us to use this principle-while we are in the midst of a practical situation in our day to day life.

The needs of this mind set are contrary

and often contradictory! While it is unavoidable to use the Natural reserves, how do we strike a balance?

To achieve this, the primary need is to have a trained mind - which can weigh all facts with utmost equanimity and devise a via media path.

Coexistence and mutual dependence are feasible only if the sovereignty of the individual is established - this is as important as the power of Nature. A weak man is no match to the Nature - especially if he has to practice co existence! So in order to develop and sustain this mind set it is imperative to have a strong personality and mind as well.

To align to this two pronged need, the Indian thinkers developed among others, a daily practice cum exercise popularly known as "sandhyavandanam". This is a daily review to ensure that our activities are in line with the above principles and to reenergize ourselves to meet with the mental needs of the following days activities.

Is this a new issue that has come up suddenly in the fast developing world? It may be true that present day activities have accelerated the need for "right mind set" but this has been the case all through the human development and civilization.

Knowing the importance of this mindset, the Indian sages have made the commencement of this practice as an essential prerequisite to the very learning process!

This practice has been set to some format and procedure. But the moot point is to understand and mull over the principles in the mind before one starts his work. The ideas to be mulled over and practiced are brought out here apart from explaining the mundane procedures.

==========

My Sandhyavandanam prayer
the theme at a glance ....

Water is the key energy needed for life. Let that be available to all of us all the time-now and in future. We will use this carefully and equitably share amongst us.

Fire is an essential need for life. It warms up and awakens the intuitive powers. Let that Fire awaken and kindle my inner energy for doing actions in my life.

Wind and earth are the other two major resources that help in my day to day life.

Sun, reigning over the sky, is the prime source of energy. It kindles the life and activity everywhere in the Universe - including humans, animals and plants.

There is a Universal Spirit that has powered all these resources and energies -water, fire, land, air, sun etc. Let these arouse the strength within me.

Let me, you and the natural forces coexist, mutually respect each other and work together. I thank the Nature for giving an uninterrupted and unfailing support.

On my part, if I have failed knowingly or unknowingly to respect

♦   *The Nature's order by either destroying or abusing Nature*

♦   *The accepted code of conduct in this physical world relating to eating, earning, wealth and enjoying due to my selfish desire and anger, Oh Supreme! Pardon me. I will endeavor to correct my future actions.*

If I am pushed to any unfair treatment in this world, you protect me.

I seek happiness here in this life and in future.

========

The above prayers:

- *Are set to a formal procedure to help us to make it part of our daily routine.*

- *Are compiled with the Veda mantras to create enough vibrations for the body and mind to remain steady.*

- *Are to be rolled over mentally within every morning, noon and evening to keep the mind peaceful.*

. *Will help us to remain course corrected in our approach to life on a day to day basis.*

- *Are common to all irrespective of gender, caste, creed or social status.*

=======

CONTENTS

I. BACKGROUND

1.1 Most of the days, when you wake up in the morning, your mother might ask you about what happened in school and also in the playground the previous day. She would like to know what were the problems faced by you and how you solved them. After listening to you, she further asks about that day's likely events and tells you how you should guard yourself in not repeating the mistakes that you made the previous day. She encourages by saying you know the way to handle and that you need to be merely conscious of your strengths. She tries to make you realize your strengths and use them.

After that, you go to school and spend the day in school, playground, tennis court, music class and get back late in the evening. Your mother again talks to you to know about the events while you were away and how you fared. This activity and dialogue between you and your mother happens at least once a day.

Why does she do that? It is with the view that you must put your best in handling the things on your own. She trains you to use your strengths and prepares you to face any situation in future.

But as you go to higher classes, your mother does not probe into all activities. She asks for only major event or exceptions. May be, when you reach college level she may do that once in week only. Does it mean that the appraisal she did when you were in lower classes is not necessary - especially when you grow? No. You have been trained by your mother over the years to examine yourself on the activities and actions you do. You do that review yourself - may be lying on the bed every night, or at breakfast table before going to school / college or office!

Take the case of your father or any adult for that matter. He does it himself every day as he is already trained to do that review. So when you grow, you might also do that.

1.2 Unfortunately, as you grow, the problems that you come across may also increase both in number and type. Say for example your father has to worry about office, house, bank, society and about you etc. These are the things that are generally manageable. Yet, there are many day to day sudden problems such as water and power shortage in the city, fire in the area, pollution, tsunami etc which make our life very difficult. Once we are faced with such issues of daily occurance, our day to day activities also come to a grinding halt. We find ourselves very helpless. Say for example, if there is a major epidemic of cholera or heavy rain in our city, we are totally lost. The life in the city is changed totally. So in effect your father must seek the support of all the natural forces, administrative forces - to carry on his daily activity. If there is any issue relating to them, he must take these into account in his action plan. So his contemplation covers not only issues relating to the family, society but also relating to the Government, the Nature and similar cosmic forces etc.

Once he knows the issue he can at least be prepared to act accordingly.

1.3 To sum up, **he reviews**

- His personal actions (physical and behavioral)
- Nature and the forces that govern the life around us

Accordingly, **he rejuvenates** himself by telling his mind that he has the strength to face and steer though the problems. By this self-assertion he gets the strengths that are needed.

1.4 What is true and applicable to you and your father is applicable to all. The underlying fact is that we need to have a composite review and self-stimulating technique - suitable for our day to day life. How do we do that? Our elders thought about this in depth. What I explained earlier (about the reviews made by your mother) is an informal way. But one must have a standard procedure to do this on a long term basis.

With the above in mind, our elders devised a review and a proactive self-stimulation technique. With that technique you get the necessary energy and drive required to face any situation in the world!

1.5 The underlying principle propounded by all elders - based on their experience - is that "whatever one intensely thinks or meditates upon - that happens / becomes". One must have this feeling and belief - in order for things to happen. Faith in yourself and the universe around you - are the important ingredients needed to face the world. Similarly with that faith you must practice this technique as well. Procedures, intellectual discussions etc are needed only to further strengthen that faith.

1.6 What is Sandhyavandanam?

It is a simple, compact and organized procedure to:

A. Carry out a mental **comprehensive** review or action replay of one's actions in the previous session of the day with a view to understand the mistakes done to oneself, fellow beings and the nature that surrounds us.

B. Reaffirm and recognize fervently the mutual dependence of man, the natural forces and energies that control our universe.

C. Recharge one's own energy to the highest level through positive thinking.

D. Thank the Natural forces around us

The above helps and ensures that we live happily, effectively and that we achieve the smooth running of the universe itself - making the world a stable and joyous platform to live.

Sandhyavandhanam is accordingly divided in two parts – Chapter V covering "A and B" and Chapter VI focusing on "C".

1.7 At this stage we get a few logical questions.

1.7.1 Is it the only way to comprehend? Is this the only way to achieve the objective? Certainly not. However this is one of the tested methods. You can start with this and improve on this based on your personal experience. But make sure that you start with something readily available as early as possible.

1.7.2 There is another logical question that would arise at this point of time. A review and self-preparation for facing the world and nature is fine. But how are we sure that there will be positive response from the other factors involved in the issue i.e. - the people around us and the nature that surrounds us. I can answer this with an example. Say, you get beaten up one day in the school bus by one of your friends. As soon as you reach home your mother asks about the details.

If she feels that your friend has been unfair in beating you, she calls up that friend's mother and appraises her on the happenings. That mother in turn talks to your friend and explains why he ought not to have reacted the way he did. So your mother "communicated" the issue to the concerned and explained, sometimes even pleaded to make sure that you don't get similar treatment in future.

If you had not communicated, these actions would not have taken place. So there is a clear need to express our needs and reactions to all concerned. While it is easy to talk to people who are around you, how do we communicate to Nature? Many of our elders worked on this and found that we can express our thoughts straight from our mind to the respective Natural force (as in the case of a direct file transer in a computer). If we focus our mind on Nature and ask that force to help, they found that help comes!! As Buddha said, "what you think, you become!" This is a hypothesis and hence can only be verified. You cannot prove it like a scientific experiment.

However, one should be sincere and truthful - in the communication. In our example, if you beat your friend everyday and report that you were beaten up, next time your mother calls up, your friend's mother will not take any action at all after speaking to your mother. **Similarly, your prayer or request is answered only if you "act" as well in the right way.** For example if you cut trees mercilessly or abuse the Nature by wrong usages, you cannot expect cooperation from Nature, however much you may pray. So prayer has to be backed by sincere and right actions.

1.7.3 The basic truth is that our mind builds the environment around us. The various scientific inventions that you see around us -for example the software Applications that you use, the supermarkets and departmental stores that you often visit - all had their birth in the mind of a person/persons as a concept. These persons had the Faith that they can create something new. So with that faith they worked hard and were able to translate those concepts into physical realities. So equipping the mind and making it realize its potential - supported by hard work - is the key to success in life. Sandhyavandhanam helps you in that direction.

1.7.4 Therefore the key three deliverables from this technique are - (1) a strong faith in yourself (2) ability to put in hard work and (3) an undoubted acceptance of the principles of mutual dependence and well being - between you, the things around you and the cosmic force.

1.7.5 Three or four centuries ago, this technique was taught as an integral part of the then conventional schools - often referred to as Vedapathashalas. In those days, Vedapathashalas in India used to teach over 184 professions to meet with the needs of life. Under the British rule, in 1835, a gentleman named Lord Macaulay devised a system on which our modern schooling is based. With this system, the study of physical sciences and the mental education got separated unintentionally. This indirectly made the Vedapathashala limit its syllabus to mere scholastic and ritualistic studies of older scriptures.

That is why, (under the Indian scenario) you are compelled to attend two "schools" -one covering the wordly physical sciences and the other covering knowledge to face the outer world. On the Upanayanam day, you are seeking admission to the second school.

We can only wish that another Lord Macaulay or Veda Vyas appears again to merge these streams of schooling! Till that time we need to continue with the "two schools" concept.

1.7.6 There are pros and cons for both the earlier system and the above modern "two school" system. Each has some good features. May be we should strike a nice balance - but being fully conscious of the scope and benefits of each system - in day to day life.

With this above background you should start learning Sandhyavandhanam.

========

Animals are always a part of Nature and they do not go against it. For example they never destroy anything to build a shelter!

II. ABOUT UPANAYANAM

2.1 What is Upanayanam and what is its significance?

Upanayanam is a function organized as a formal occasion to teach you the Sandhya - vandhanam. You should follow that and use it for your benefit. Since it is an important landmark in your life - as you are about to learn a technique that is going to help you throughout your life it is formally celebrated. Upanayanam literally means "taking you near". Till that day you were totally under the cover and protection of your father and mother. That day they are going to initiate you to face life - i.e. take you near real life. This is also symbolically done during the function.

The function has three symbolic stages:

Mother is the first teacher to anyone. She is given the status of the First Guru. She inaugurates this function wih the words:

▶▶▶▶

"My son, treat every woman as your mother until you are twenty four. Maintain the celibacy till marriage. Engage your mind in studying the scriptures and meditate on the Gayatri mantra which will be imparted to you later today. May that Universal Mother protect you throughout your life".

Then the formal Guru (normally a priest) blesses you with the thread. Then your father imparts the mantra and technique to you.

It is for you to learn and use the same in your life.

This is also called Brahmopadesam - instruction about the Nature and the universal spirit. This technique will eventually take you to the understanding of the "cosmos" as such and your role in it.

When you were admitted to the school -you were initiated to education and worldly knowledge - to help you to earn. This admission has a larger connotation. You are formally admitted to the "school of life".

Upanayanam is a 'knowledge' ceremony, which was used to initiate the process of learning, knowledge and evolution of intelligence. However Upanayanam has become a 'social' festival these days with lot of style and pomp. In reality, it is of equal value whether done in a grand manner or only as a small gathering within your family.

2.2 Upanayanam is only a formal ceremonial start. The education and instructions are only initiated. It has to be continued regularly. On this day you are given four things:

A. A badge:

You are primarily initiated to the technique. Once you are initiated you are given a badge. It is like giving a "test cap" to one in cricket. Like the cap you are given the "poonal" as a badge. Merely qualifying / wearing the cap do not make you a good player. You need to practice and perform consistently. Similarly this "life cap" is given to you - but it is for you to practice and perform accordingly.

B. Formal inclusion in a "House" or group.

Just as an entrant to school is assigned to the "Blue House" or "Red House" of a school, you will be formally assigned to a house - i.e. to the House to which your father belongs. The "house" is identified by two things: It covers:

♦ *Pravara and Gotra*

♦ *Sutra (Kalpa) and Shaaka*

♦ ***Pravara and Gotra:*** Some Rishis collectively started this particular "house". These Rishis are generally called "pravaras". It is customary to specify either three or five pravaras. Persons who is the descendent of each Pravara is identified by a Gotra. The Gotra normally carries the name of one of the Pravara Rishi himself e.g. Bharatwaja Gotra etc.

♦ ***Sutra and Sakha:*** They specify the subject that you plan to take up for study and specialization. This is done based on what

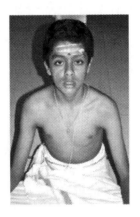

What is the Universal Spirit?

Invariably everyone will agree that there is one driving force which runs / controls the Universe. You may call it "God", "Universal energy" or "Brahman" or by any other name. To best of human knowledge that controls and ensures the smooth running of this cosmos - as we see and experience it today. That supreme energy is referred to as "universal spirit".

▶▶ ▶▶

you are good at , for example - singing / prayer (Rig), doing some activity/investigations of world around us (Yajur), in poetry and fine arts (Sama) or in Worldly sciences and arts (Atharva).

The sakha also specifies the particular school to which you belong. In the olden days the offspring took the same subject taken by his father. That tradition still continues at least in this area. You are allowed to study and specialize in the other areas as well - but generally after you have covered and mastered your own sakha.

C. You are administered an oath

On that day, When you wear the thread you take an oath. The oath is to formally accept (a) the allegiance to your House and (b) to work as per the order of the Universe - for the benefit of all - i.e. you, fellow men, animals, plants and the cosmic forces.

The oath:

यज्ञोपवीतं परमं पवित्रं प्रजापतेर्यत् सहजं
पुरस्तात् । आयुष्यमग्रियं प्रतिमुंच शुभ्रं
यज्ञोपवीतं बलमस्तु तेजः ॥

*Yagnopavitam   paramam   pavitram
Prajaapatheryatsahajam purastaat, aayushyam
agryam pratimuncha   shubram   yagno
pavitam   balamastu thejah.*

"The meaning as follows : Put on this sacrificial thread which is supremely sacred, which became manifest long ago with Prajapati, (the first created being) and which embodies longevity, eminence and purity May it bring strength to me."

See Section VIII. 2 for the full procedure that is followed to wear or replace a yagyopavitam/poonal.

D. A Few Symbolic actions to say that you are free to face the world of knowledge, responsibility and duties.

Asmaarohanam - standing on the stone - ceremony is performed. You are made to place your right foot on a piece of rock so that your willpower will be like a rock and that you can face anything with determination. The teacher asks you to recite the following mantra which means -"be firm and strong like this stone". The stone stands for strength and the ability to withstand anything. The **ritual is** symbolic of not being affected by the problems of life and to win over all internal enemies.

Kumaara bhojanam - to emphasise that the boy should learn to live, eat with his fellow students. The boy eats with his friends and peers.

Taking bikshaa: A symbolic ceremony to show that the boy has to manage himself with the food given by others in contrast to "being fed by mother – alone and regularly". He gets a new identification starting with the word "abhivadhaya" and that is first recited to his mother. Mother also initiates the act of taking biksha, by giving the first biksha to her son. Apart from being given the status to inaugurate the day's proceedings, it is the mother who ensures that the boy presents himself properly to the outside world. That is the importance given to motherhood.

Solemn Vow: The function marks your entrance into the life as a student and the acceptance by others in the community. The occassion is so solemn that then the boy is declared as "dvija" or "born again". The boy takes a vow that he would become capable of performing his duties and responsibilities on his own. The vow goes as follows: "Let us meditate on the light of the sun which represents God, and may our thoughts be inspired by that divine light".

III.   SOME MORE DETAILS RELATING TO SANDHYAA VANDANAM

3.1. When to do Sandhyaavandanam?

It is like asking how many times the captain of the cricket team should consult and review with his team mates the strategy for proceeding with the game, while the game is in progress. You would definitely agree that he needs to ask whenever there is a need. However to ensure that the game is not stopped too many times in this type of formal consultation, official "strategic break time" is allotted. Similarly one can practice this technique when ever there is a need in the course of one's activities. However for the sake of order it is recommended to be done thrice a day - i.e. at the beginning, end and middle of every day - to ensure that one is charged to his capacity at all times to act. This acts as "recharging" of one's battery.

Since the basic objective is to achieve and ensure the welfare of the fellow men and creatures to ensure smooth running of our universe it is universal in content and spirit.

> *The prayer is composed in such a manner that this can be followed by anyone irrespective of the caste, creed Social status or gender.*

3.2. What is the objective of Doing Sandhayaa Vandanam?

This prepares one to face the world and to act confidently that too on a day to day basis.

In short, these Sandhyaavandanam mantras - exhort a person to radiate fearlessly by invoking the energy in them. The whole purpose of learning is to become fearless enough to radiate what we have. People who have learnt this truth will become fearless and radiate what they have, whether it is wealth, knowledge or more importantly the confidence of facing life.

3.3. When and who can Start Doing Sandhayaa Vandanam?

Since this involves a larger principle in life this can be done only after one reaches an age of ten and above ie after the boy stabilizes in the first school.

As per the established convention, a Brahmin child's Upanayanam is generally performed when he is eight years old from conception that is when he is seven years and two months old from birth. A Kshatriya's is to be performed at the age of twelve. The corresponding age for a Vaisya is sixteen. There is no mention about the Shudras in this regard.

In olden days Shudras referred to those who were engaged in manual labour - big or small. (It was not a classification by birth). As their work involved primarily dealing with the maintenance, upkeep and preservation of Nature - they needed no exclusive time for praying. Their work itself was a prayer and commitment to Nature.

> *In olden days girls also had Upanayanam. But the practice was discontinued for no definite and spelt out reason. It is interesting to note that, Sita performed Sandhyavandan (even in the days she was kept in captivity) and the same is explicitly brought out in the SundaraKaandam of Valmiki.*

These age factor was fixed a few centuries ago when the Upanayanam was also coinciding with the start of your formal education. In today's context, since the formal start of education is decided and controlled by the rules of the government / educational system it is acceptable to start by at least ten.

3.4. How this is to be done?

There are around fourteen prayers in Part I and eleven in Part II - (totally twenty, excluding the mantras that are repeated) each two or three lines - they will take only five minutes. One has to focus and work on those thoughts brought out in the prayers with full attention. Technically, this process of Sandhyavandanam can be done in any random fashion to get the full effect.

3.5. Why follow the Procedure and not restrict to Prayer alone?

One may find it very difficult to focus intently on the thoughts brought out in these prayers. So to make it easy for beginners, they are cogently linked in the form of a formal procedure.

3.6. Is There any benefit by adopting this procedure and not limiting to just the prayer?

The prayers are linked through a procedure. The prayers are said adopting certain techniques -

1) Formal chanting (praise),

2) Pranayaam
   (Yogic breathing - breadth control),

3) Token offerings (tarpan) and

4) A few body actions / activities
   (salutations,) and

5) Self energizing (anga vandana).

All these methods are found by experience to get "mind control". Hence one is exposed to all methods - to enable one to select the most suited one.

3.7. What is the Significance of the "thread" that is adorned?

As the objective of Sandhyavandhanam is **"universal welfare and wellbeing"** you are proudly joining the brigade that is working for not only for individual success but also for success and welfare of the fellow beings, animals, plants. As a mark of joining this club you are given the *badge - "thread"* - that you formally start wearing from that day.

3.8. Is there any levels in this study and practice?

On admission, you wear three strings. Once the student achieves a certain level of knowledge, the guru adds three more strings signifying "graduation" and there after the student goes on for higher studies. He generally decides to travel (Yatra) to Kashi (in north India) to pursue higher education. At this point, the father of the potential bride convinces the youth to get married and then go to Kashi with his bride. As the above concept is not very much valid in the present day system, the addition of the three more strings is followed by *"Kashi Yatra"* in South Indian wedding ceremonies. In modern days, the ceremony *(Kashi Yatra)* is packaged as if it is a part of the wedding!

3.9. What to do under present day time constraints?

It is recommended that you do the both Part one and two - the entire procedure – thrice a day.

> *If you are not in a position to do, either chant the Mantras or roll over the underlying thoughts in the mind - with 100% concentration on it.*

IV *A few Special* *Features of Sandhyaavandanam?*

♦ This is a common "entry exercise" to life and is applicable to all. Once you learn this technique, you are equipped to work and achieve success in pure worldly life, pure spiritual life or in a balanced life combining both.

♦ The procedure adopts the best texts from the Vedas / Upanishads to draw its pattern and organizing the sequence of the practice. There are passages starting from Agnihotra (a daily ritual done) upto Aswamedhayaga (done by king for the welfare of the nation and their kingdom). They are cut and pasted in the Sandhyavandhanam procedure.

♦ While delivering the mantras, the various known practices are used as a medium so that once you follow the sequence, you touch upon each practice everyday. It incorporates breathing exercise, basic yoga postures, chanting, praise, describing the beauty in a poetical fervor etc. They are just touched upon with a view to enable you to know the overall pastures and select what suits you the best personally for detailed study.

♦ This practice has passages that cover your personal and universal welfare. The rendering of these on a daily basis makes you feel important in society and ready to face your life.

♦ The composition of the practice is such that even if you don't understand the full meaning etc it is beneficial. However if you understand and do it the benefits are better absorbed by you.

♦ It is called a Nitya karma whose objective is to bring about self purification and attunement to cosmic creation. As a result of daily practice the mind is made pure, its present weakness and inertia are eliminated and its full power is manifested. It is a wonderful mental exercise to elevate and equip the mind for the purpose of life in totality.

♦ It incorporates the elements or features of the four main types of Yoga (Karma, Bhakthi, Dhyana and Jnana).

♦ While doing Sandhyavandanam, two set of phrases are repeated a number of times: They are Om (the sound representation of the primeval energy) and Vyahrutis. Vyahrutis represent the creation around you. (Refer to 6.7 for details). As mentioned earlier, Sandhyavandanam is a conference call between you, the forces around you and the Supreme Being. Often you may get distracted while you are on this call. To bring your mind back to the conversation, you address them (the other parties in the conference call) repeatedly either direct or while doing any other activity.

========

A moment please ....before you go further into the practice of Sandhya vandhanam

Faith is the vision of the soul - the power by which spiritual things are apprehended, just as material things are apprehended by physical senses.

With total faith, you go through the practice of Sandhya vandhanam - which will help in two ways

♦ You get trained to hear the inner voice clearly, even when you are in the midst of a practical situation your life

♦ Your energy to ACT will be at its best levels at all times throughout the day.

Equipped with the above - the ability to hear the inner voice and your energy level at its best - you will be able to face the challenges of the world successfully.With that energy you are ready to chart your destiny the way you want.

With this open mind, faith, devotion - go through this practice ....

V. Sandhyaa Vandanam

There are 14 steps covered by 11 mantras. The gist of the same is given. The procedure is summarised in the following pages.

The procedure varies slightly for the followers of Rig / Yajur / Sama and Atharva Vedas. (However the basic mantras and concepts are the same). The procedures detailed are based on the practices followed in Yajur Veda.

Part V is to be performed by sitting down - facing east in the morning or north in the evening.

=========

▶▶▶▶

Mantra 1	*Purify your body to practice this technique*
Mantra 2	*Pray that there should be no hindrance while you practice this technique.*
Mantra 3	*Focus the mind by doing a breathing exercise*
Mantra 4	*Be sure and aware that you are doing this practice not only for your self but for all people, animals, plants and the Nature around you (Sankalpa)*
Mantra 5	*Acknowledge that Water is the main source of life and very existence. Pray to the Supreme for and its abundant supply. Also assure that you will use this source with care and equitably among you all.*

Mantra 6	*This is a prayer over which you review your actions and confess the mistakes (done by not conforming to the cosmic order and rules) to the Universal spirit with a request to exonerate you.*
Mantra 7	*Now, you purify yourself again as you psychologically feel relieved of the ill effects of your past action, by reciting mantra 6.*
Mantra 8	*Feel more receptive and ask for the good effects to be bestowed and handed over to you fast. You pray to Agni (fire), the betower of aspiration in life. You get prepared to meet with the day to day challenges.*
Mantra 9	*After this review you want to show your care in your own small way for Him (The Universal Spirit) by offering water as a token – offered three times.*

Mantra 9 Continued

This is your reconfirmation of faith and solidarity towards the sun, planets and their order.

Mantra 10

It is recommended that that you do this review thrice a day – so that you can course correct your actions at short intervals. Sometimes, due to various reasons you might not have done the same. As a compensation you are giving one more offering.

Mantra 11

After the review process you recharge yourself mentally by dwelling on the thought that you are part of that Universal Spirit and hence you long for the needed energy. You should only realize it and use. You pray to the Universal spirit to remove the limitations on your personality.

Mantra 12	*Purify yourself and feel energized.*
Mantra 13	*Acknowledge the services of all secondary forces in the universe and thank them by offering water as a token of your gratitude.*
Mantra 14	*Close the practice*

Perform Achamanam

Meaning: As a first step carry out self purifying and energizing with water and stimulate the body with "acupressure like touches", saying twelve holy names. While touching, mentally seek the protection of various limbs in the body and remind yourself that these limbs are energized for your life mission.

When mantras or the names of the Supreme Energy are recited with focused mind, positive vibrations are generated. Water has the property to hold the energy generated by such vibrations. That energized water is taken in small quantities to rejuvenate the body. The same water is also sprinkled externally over the body, head, limbs etc to energise them by infusion technique.

Different types and forms of energies are required to protect us over each month of the year – depending upon the ambience, weather etc. So also the various limbs need different forms of energies. These forms of energies are labelled as different names used here.

Procedure: Take small quantities of water three times in the right hand and swallow it while reciting the following mantra.

Mantra:

अच्युताय नमः । अनन्ताय नमः ।
गोविन्दाय नमः ।

Om Achyuthaaya namaha, Om Ananthaaya namaha Om Govindaaya namaha

केशव । नारायण । माधव । गोविन्द ।
विष्णो । मधुसूदन । त्रिविक्रम । वामन ।
श्रीधर । हृषीकेश । पद्मनाभ । दामोदर ।।

Then touch with thumb both cheeks saying   Kesava - Narayana

Touch with ring finger both eyes saying Madhava - Govinda

Touch with the first finger both sides of nose saying Vishno - Madhusoodana Touch with little finger both ears saying Trivikrama - Vamana Touch with the middle finger both shoulders saying Sreedhara - Hrishikesa

Touch with all fingers the belly button saying Padmanabha

Touch with all fingers the head saying Damodara

2. Dhyanam

Meaning: I meditate on him (The Universal Spirit) - one who is clad in white, who is present everywhere, who has four hands, who is always pleasant to look at - with a prayer that in the process undertaken by me, I should not face any hurdles. (While it is being done).

Procedure: Recite the following mantra slowly tapping the forehead with both fists together. (Tapping is symbolic of alerting the mind to get focussed on the ensuing activities).

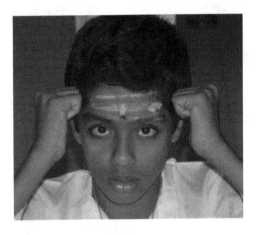

Mantra:

गणपति-ध्यानम् ॥२॥

शुक्लाम्बरधरं विष्णुं शशिवर्णं चतुर्भुजम् ।

प्रसन्नवदनं ध्यायेत् सर्व-विघ्नोपशान्तये ॥

Shuklambaradharam Vishnum Sasi Varnam Chathur Bhujam, Prasanna Vadanam Dyayeth Sarva Vigna Upa Santhaye.

3. Praanaayaamam

This is done with a view to establish a psycho-somatic harmony. Pranayamam is based on the following principle: When the thoughts are focused breathing is slow and rhythmic. In the same way when the breathing is made rhythmic and slow - thoughts will be focused.

"How is it that if you control your breath, the mind will be still?" We see that when the mind is still the breath also stops. When our wonder is aroused, when we are grief-stricken or when we are overjoyed, the mind becomes one-pointed. We exclaim *"Ha"* and the breath stops for a moment. But soon we breathe fast. We do not stop breathing with any effort on our part-the stopping is involuntary. The mind stops when it is enwrapped or absorbed in something. Then we heave a sigh-take a long breath-making up for the momentary stoppage of breathing. We learn from this that, when breathing momentarily stops, the mind becomes one-pointed. This is the reason why the breath is controlled when arghya, libation, is offered.

Kanchi Paramacharya

Meaning: Bhoo to Sathya - represent the seven vyahruties and are also refered to as the seven lokas. These energy bands run the universe the way it is running. The Universal spirit (which is above all these) is adorable and is the ultimate controller of all these lokas/energy bands. Let that same spirit energize me also. This is a prayer to the cosmic world, to bless and bring all good things, for the benefit of all, from all sides, directions and lokas.

Procedure: This is done using the pranayama technique. Hold both Nostrils with Thumb and the little and third finger of the hands and recite.Inhale while reciting (!), hold while reciting (!!) and exhale while reciting (!!!)

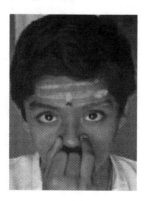

Mantra:

(!)ओं भूः । ओं भुवः । ओꣳ सुवः ।

ओं महः । ओं जनः। ओं तपः ।

ओꣳसत्यम् ।। (!)

(!!)ओं तत् सवितुर्वरेण्यं भर्गो देवस्य

धीमहि । धियो यो नः प्रचोदयात् ।।(!!)

(!!!) ओमापो-ज्योती-रसोऽमृतं-ब्रह्म

भूर्भुवस्सुवरोम् ।। (!!!)

Om Bhoo Om Bhuva Ogum Suva
Om Maha Om Jana Om Thapa
Ogum Sathyam Om Tatsa vithur
varenyam
Bargo devasya dhi mahi dhiyo yonah
Prachodayaath Om Apaha Jyothi
Rasaha Amrutham brahma
Bhoorbuvasuvarom

Sankalpa - *Means a wish to commune with the universal energy.*

---

4. Sankalpam

Meaning: Sankalpam reaffirms the definite, determined and clear intention for carrying out this activity.

I am carrying out Sandhya vandanam in the morning with a focused mind and in the spirit of true analysis. I am doing this (a) to get rid of all bad effects accrued to me due to my actions (b) to show my support in fulfilling the aspirations of the Supreme spirit.

This spells out our confidence that we too are a part of that Supreme Spirit in running this cosmos.

The Universal spirit has its own plan that is unknown to us. We pray that whatever we do should only be a support to that working.

Procedure:

Keep the right palm inside the left palm and keep the palms on the right thigh and recite.

Mantra:

संकल्पः ॥४॥

ममोपात्त-समस्त-दुरित-क्षय-द्वारा-श्रीपरमेश्वर-प्रीत्यर्थं

In the morning say   प्रातः सन्ध्या-मुपासिष्ये ॥

At noon say   माध्यान्हिकं करिष्ये ॥

In Evening say   सायं सन्ध्या-मुपासिष्ये ॥

Mamo paththa samastha duritha kshaya dwara, Sri Parameshwara preethyartham, pratha sandhyaam upaasishye (for madhyannikam say madhyaynikam karishye and in the evening say "sayam sandhyam upaasishye")

1, 2, *3 and 4 are generally followed before carrying out any spiritual or religious activity. This is to reiterate to yourself that all activities have to be carried out in a spirit of mutual dependance   & coexistence.*

The *significance of the preparatory steps 1 to 4 followed in the communication process between humans and the Supreme Power*

1. Achamana: It is the process of cleansing and energising yourself before starting any prayer or activity. It is akin to the modern "freshening up" before starting any serious work. This ensures physical alertness to what you want to do. The acupressure touches that is followed emphasises the need to be physically alert during the communication process.

2. After Achamana you do a general prayer to ensure that no major hindrances come on the way while completing this task just undertaken.

▶▶▶▶

This is addressed to Lord Ganesh -protector from all hurdles.

3. Om - The Pranava Mantra. The Pranava Mantra "om" is the carrier wave used in the communication between human beings and The Supreme Energy. The carrier wave is generated by us. The messages that we want to convey (either in the form of a prayer/request/praise) is mounted on the wave. The process is similar to modulation technique in communication. Such modulation helps to cross through the various frequency bands - before reaching the Supreme Power. The response to this prayer / request also comes back through the same wave (by way of intuition) back to the humans -though it may come at a different point of time.

How do we mount the message on to the carrier wave? A focussed mind has the power to push the message on to the carrier wave zand also hrough various frequency bands - Bhur …..to..…sathyam. This process is commonly known as Praanaayaama.

Since one wants to ensure that the message is mounted and remain so - all through - we constantly repeat "Om Bhur ......Om sathyam" often during the process of our prayers.

5. *Sankalpa (resolve):* In simple terms, Sankalpa is nothing but a resolution stating the "wish list" that you convey to the Supreme power formally. It also conveys to the Supreme power that you are wanting this message to be definitely considered. If the wishes are sincere, reasonable and positive in nature they are likely to be answered and fulfilled.

The words like "parameswara preethyartham" clearly emphasises that we are more concerned about the cosmic order than any personal gains.

Mantras 1, 2, 3 and 4 are the ones that cover this preparation. This is followed before doing - Part I, Part II and Part III.

▶▶▶▶

5. *Marjanam*

(Cleansing)

You start the practice by praying to the source which is a basic need for very existence - i.e. water

Meaning: Energize by sprinkling water on yourself. This invokes all the water on the earth. Water is needed for the start and sustenance of all life. You become aware of this and acknowledge it formally.

This para, though it appears like a mere prayer, is a commitment made by you to use the available water discreetly and also to share this valuable resource equitably with your fellow human beings.

Procedure: Take a spoonful of water, Say "Sri kesavaya namaha" (write OM in water with the ring finger). Recite the following ten short sentences. While reciting the first seven lines sprinkle water on the head, while reciting the

Eighth line touch the feet, nineth sprinkle on the head and complete by reciting the tenth with taking little water on your right palm and sprinkling around your head in clockwise direction. (It is also referred to as Atma parishechanam). By sprinkiling water one infuses energy to various limbs.

Sankalpa - *converts the dynamic mental force of willpower "iccha Shakti" into a living entity.*

Swami Sathyananda Saraswathi

▶▶▶▶

Meaning:

There are 9 parts to this mantra

Om Kesavaya namah	my salutations to Kesava
Aapo hishta mayo bhuva	Water is needed to take care of our welfare and hence Water is indeed adorable.
Thana oorje dadha thana	Water gives the energy
Mahe ranaaya chakshase	Water is like the eye of the Universal spirit so that we can have the vision of universal spirit.

Yova shiva thamo rasa	This is the elixir of life
Thasya bhajaya thehana	I must get water here today
Usatheeriva mataraha	To be distributed and used just as a mother would allocate the available resources to her progenies.
Thasma aranga mamava	Be available wherever I go
Yasya kshayaya jinwadha	Bestow on us the boon of a next life sanctified by knowledge
Aapo janayatha chanaha	Oh Water, bless us

Om bhur-bhuva suvah

Mantra:

मार्जनम् ३॥ ५॥

ओं श्रीकेशवाय नमः ॥

आपो हि ष्ठा मयो भुवः ॥१॥

ता न ऊर्जे दधातन ॥२॥

महे रणाय चक्षसे ॥३॥

यो वः शिवतमो रसः ॥४॥

तस्य भाजयतेह नः ॥५॥

उशतीरिव मातरः ॥६॥

तस्मा अरं गमाम वः ॥७॥

यस्य क्षयाय जिन्वथ ॥८॥

आपो जनयथा च नः ॥९॥

ओं भूर्भुवस्सुवः ॥१०॥

(आत्म-परिषेचनम्) ॥

[3]This mantra is taken from Rig Veda (RV) 7.6.5 /
Taitreeya Aranyaka (TA) 4.1.5.

6. Praasanam

This is a prayer over which one reviews his actions and confesses the mistakes to The Universal spirit with a request to exonerate him. The mantras are different for the three sessions. Since the activities are different during the course of the day, the mantras also cover the possible areas of faults in those activities. For example in the night it would be family related interactions and activities, where as during the day business and commerce related activities may be predominant.

Morning Prayer (Pratha sandhya)

Meaning:

I resort to wrong actions either due to anger or arising out of pent up anger. Let Sun Exonerate and protect me from such misdeeds done in the night. The misdeeds done could be by mind, word, hand, leg, stomach or genitals. Whatever was done by me, I am truthfully offering to you through this water (This is a token of my sincere submission) and please accept this offering. Once exonerated I offer myself to sun-as an offering (I am committing my self to work for the cosmic cause.)

Procedure: Take small quantity of water in the palm, recite the following mantha and drink it while telling "swaha". The procedure is same for pratha -sandhya, madhyanhika and sayam sandhya.

Mantra:

प्राशनम् ॥६॥

प्रातः - सूर्यश्च मा मन्युश्च मन्युपतयश्च मन्युकृतेभ्यः । पापेभ्यो रक्षन्ताम् । यद्रात्र्या पापमकार्षम् । मनसा वाचा हस्ताभ्याम् । पद्भ्या-मुदरेण शिश्ना । रात्रि-स्तदवलुंपतु । यत्किंच दुरितं मयि । इदमहं मामामृत-योनौ ।

सूर्ये ज्योतिषि जुहोमि स्वाहा ॥६.१॥[4]

Sooryascha ma manyuscha manyu patayascha manyukruthebhyaha Paapebhyo rakshantham. Yad rathrya papa ma karsham. Manasa vacha

[4]Taken from Taitreeya Aranyaka 10.32

Hasthabhyam. Padbhyaam udarena sisnaa Rathri sthadha valumpathu. Yad kincha duritham mayi. Idhamaham maam amruta yonau. Soorye jyothishi juhomi swaahaa

Prayer at Noon (Madhyanhika)

Meaning:

Water energises and cleanses the earth and those arising out of earth. Water is also one of the forms of energy of the Universal Spirit. Let that Water energise me and my teacher/guide as well. Let this awareness and knowledge (Veda) cleanse me.

If I have eaten anything non edible or which is not good to be eaten or any thing left out by others, purify me. If I had been conducting badly and had accepted any return not in proportion to my work, you save me. I give myself as offering to you. May the waters purify me!

मध्याह्ने - आप : पुनन्तु पृथिवीं पृथिवी
पूता पुनातु माम् । पुनन्तु ब्रह्मण-
स्पतिर्ब्रह्म-पूता पुनातु माम् ।
यदुच्छिष्ट-मभौज्यं यद्वा दुश्चरितं मम ।
सर्वं पुनन्तु मामापोऽसतां च प्रतिग्रहँ
स्वाहा ॥ ६.२॥ [5]

Aapa punanthu prithweem, prithwee
poothaa punaathu maam. Punanthu
brahmanaspathir brahma pootha punathu
maam. Yad uchishtamabhojyam yadhwaa
ducharitham mama Sarvam punanthu
mamaapo asatham ca prathigrahagra
swaahaaha

Evening Prayer (sayam sandhya) Meaning:

The meaning is similar to the Morning
Prayer and offering as well. But this is addressed
to Fire (which is a symbol of aspiration and
action)

[5]Taitreeya Aranyaka 10.30

Swaha means "please accept my offering / donation"

May the Fire God destroy my sins done due to anger. May the presiding deity over the day destroy any sins I have committed through thought, word, deed or through food, sex or any reason. I offer all my bad acts in the mystic fire of the Supreme. May I be purified?

सायंकाले - अग्निश्च मा मन्युश्चमन्युपतयश्च
मन्युंकृतेभ्यः । पापेभ्यो रक्षन्ताम् । यदह्ना
पार्पमकार्षम् । मनसा वाचा हस्ताभ्याम् ।
पद्भ्या-मुदरेण शिश्ना । अहस्तदवलुंपतु ।
यत्किंच दुरितं मयि । इदमहं माममृतयोनौ ।
सत्ये ज्योतिषि जुहोमि स्वाहा ॥६.३॥[6]

Agnisca maa manyusca manyu patayasca
manyu kruthebhyaha Papebhyo
rakshanthaam. Yadanha paapama kaarsham.
Manasaa vaacaa hastaabhyaam.

[6]Taitreeya Aranyaka 10.31

Padbhyam udarena sisna Ahasthada valum
pathu. Yad kincha duritham mayi
Idamaham maam amruta yonau Satye
jyothishi juhomi swaahaa

7. Achamanam

Use the same mantras and action as given
under 1.You purify yourself again, as you
psychologically feel relieved now of the ill
effects of your past actions, if any. (Through the
earlier Praasanam No 6)

आचमनम् ।। 8.

Punar maarjanam

This prayer is addressed to a form of Agni
- Dhadhikravin (a horse). Agni is the symbol of
"aspiration and life force".You pray to him to
give you the needed "aspiration to work and
perform".

▶▶▶▶

Meaning: Let Dhadhikravin come as fast as possible on the horse and deliver the goodies / blessings to me. Let him make my face and mouth smell nicely. (May he endow our bodies with all perfect felicities). Let him give the benefit of long life.

Procedure: Take little water on your right palm and sprinkle on your head and around your head in clockwise. (Atma parishechanam).

Mantra:

पुनर्मार्जनम् ॥७॥

दधिक्राव्णो अकारिषम् । जिष्णो-रश्वस्य

वाजिनः । सुरभि नो मुखाकरत ।

प्रण आयूँषि तारिषत् ॥[7]

आपो हि ष्ठा मयो भुवः ।

ता न ऊर्जे दधातन । महे रणाय चक्षसे ।

[7]Taitreeya Samhita (1.5.11)

यो वः शिवतमो रसः । तस्य भाजयतेह नः ।
उशतीरिव मातरः । तस्मा अरं गमाम वः ।
यस्य क्षयाय जिन्वथ । आपो जनयथा च नः॥
ओं भूर्भुवस्सुवः ॥ (आत्म-परिषेचनम्) ॥

(4.1.5)

Dadhi kravinno akarisham. Jishno raswasya vajinaha. Surabhino mukhaa karath. Prana ayugumshi thaarishath.

Aapo hishthaa mayo bhuva, Taana oorje dadha tana, Mahe ranaaya chakshase, Yova shiva thamo rasaha. Tasya bhaajayathehanaha. Usatheeriva matharaha Thasma aranga mamava. Yasya kshayaayajinwata, Aapo janayadha janaha Om bhorbuvassuvaha.

▶▶▶▶

9. *Argya Pradhanam (Offer)*

Meaning: After the review of your activities you want to show your care (in your own small way) by offering the Universal spirit water as a token. This is our reconfirmation of faith and solidarity towards the sun and the planets to follow the rhythmic order without any conflict.

Arghyam is also a reminder of the Brahman in us and its honouring by the offer of mantra and water.

Procedure: Join both hands together and take hand full of water. (Facing east during Pratha Sandhya, facing north during Madya -nnikam, and facing west during Sayam Sandhya) repeat the following manthra and pour it. (Thrice during pratha sandhya, twice during Madhyannikam and thrice during Sayam Sandhya)

Mantra :

अर्घ्य-प्रदानम् ।।८।।

ओं भूर्भुवस्सुवं । तत् सवितु-र्वरेण्यं

भर्गो देवस्य धीमहि । धियो यो नः
प्रचोदयात् ।।

(प्रातः-३ ।। मध्याह्ने-२ ।। सायं-३ ।।)८

Om Bhorbuvassuva. Tatsa vithur varenyam
bhargo devasya deemahi.

Dhiyo yona prachodayaat.

[8]Rig veda 3.62.10, Yajur (TA) 35.9 and Sama
veda 1462.

10. Prayaschitha Argyam

Do Pranayama. (As per no.3 above).

Due to various reasons you might have missed these formal review sessions earlier. As an atonement you are giving one more offering in a similar fashion as before.

Procedure: Take small quantity of water in the right hand and move it above one's own head saying Om Bhurbhuvassuvaha. (This is called Athma parishechanam)

प्रायश्चित्तार्घ्यम् ॥९॥
प्राणायाम ॥
ओं भूर्भुवस्सुवः+धियो यो नः प्रचोदयात् ॥
ओं भूर्भुवस्सुवः ॥
(आत्मप्रदक्षिणं परिषेचनं च) ॥

Do Pranayama.

Om Bhorbuvassuva. Tatsa vithur varenyam bhargo devasya deemahi. Dhiyo yona Prachodayath

11. Ikyaanusandhanam[9]

Meaning: After the review process you recharge mentally by dwelling on the thought that you are part of that Universal Spirit and hence you can realize and use the needed energy from within. You pray to remove the limitations on your personality. This is an auto suggestion excercise.

The sun is the supreme energy and the same energy is within me as well.

[9]Is also known as Aham graha Upasana

Procedure: With both hands touch the middle of the chest. Close the eyes meditate and Chant. Dwell upon the mantra for some time to recharge yourself. (Fully realizing that you have immense power to face and act in the world)

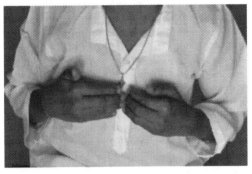

Mantra :

ऐक्यानुसन्धानम् ॥१०॥
असावादित्यो ब्रह्म । ब्रह्मैवाहमस्मि ॥
(ध्यानम् ॥ आचमनम् ॥)

Asaavadhityo Brahma. Brahmaivahamasmi

Once you believe in yourelf, you will further realise that, the kingdom of God of which prophets speak is not here or there but is in the hearts of men.

Man has the same potential as Gods. He has only to realise and act accordingly.

This also reiterates the principle that -gods are immortal men and men are mortal gods. This thought we roll over in our mind several times - in different ways and this would give the necessary strength to invoke the power within us to face the world.

12. Then do Achamanam as per 1

13. Deva Tharpanam देव तर्पणम

Meaning: This part is composed in the format of a "vote of thanks" offered in the present day world. Here we thank every form of force in this cosmic world for supporting us.

I thank the Sun, Moon, Mars, Mercury, Jupiter, Venus, Saturn, Rahu and Kethu, I satisfy Lord Kesava, Narayana, Madhava, Govinda, Vishnu, Madhusoodhana, Trivikrama, Vamana, Sreedhara, Hrishikesa, Padmanabha and Damodhara

Procedure: Sit facing east during pratha sandhya, facing north during madhyannikam, and facing east during sayam sandhya, take water in the hand and pour it out through its tips after each mantra when you say "tharpayaami". Take water separately each time.

Mantra :

आदित्यं तर्पयामि । सोमं तर्पयामि ।
अंगारकं तर्पयामि । बुधं तर्पयामि ।
बृहस्पतिं तर्पयामि । शुक्रं तर्पयामि ।
शनैश्चरं तर्पयामि । राहुं तर्पयामि ।
केतुं तर्पयामि ॥
केशवं तर्पयामि । नारायणं तर्पयामि ।
माधवं तर्पयामि । गोविन्दं तर्पयामि ॥
विष्णुं तर्पयामि । मधुसूदनं तर्पयामि ।
त्रिविक्रमं तर्पयामि । वामनं तर्पयामि ॥
श्रीधरं तर्पयामि । हृषीकेशं तर्पयामि ।
पद्मनाभं तर्पयामि । दामोतरं तर्पयामि ॥
(आचमनम् ॥) इति सन्ध्यावन्दन-पूर्वभागः ॥

Aadithyam, Somam, Angaarakam,

Budham, Brahaspathim, Shukram,

Sanaiswaram, Rahum, Kethum Kesavam,

Narayanam, Madhavam, Govindam

Vishnum, Madhusoodhanam,

Trivikramam, Vaamanam, Sreedharam,

Hrishikesam, Padmanaabham,

Damodharam - tharpayaami

14. Then do aachamanam

This ends the first part of Sandhya vandhanam.

==========

> *Mantra is not the name of a god or goddess or a person. It is not a holy word or part of a hymn. Mantra is not sacred nor is it a tool for concentration. It is a vehicle for expansion of mind and the liberation of energy.*
>
> **Swami**
> **Sathyananda**

VI. Gaayathri Japam

There are additional 11 set of mantras. The gist of the same and the procedure for the reenergizing are shown in the following pages.

============

Mantra 1:	*Pray that there should be no hindrance while you do this practice.*
Mantra 2:	*Focus the mind by doing a breathing exercise*
Mantra 3:	*Be sure that you are doing this practice for the benefit of you, all people, animals, plants and the Nature around you*
Mantra 4	*Get prepared to initiate the direct communication witth the Supreme Energy through the first portion of the Gayatri mantra by emembering the Rishi who gave the mantra, the metre of the mantra and the devatas on whom they are addressed*
Mantra 5	** Do pranayama 10 times Contemplating on the mantra*

▶▶▶▶

Mantra 6	*Re assure yourself that divine force is with in you and experience that force in you (by reciting and doing the Avahanam)*
Mantra 7	*Pray and contemplate on the Gayatri mantra as many times - as time permits. Liberate the energy within you.*
Mantra 8	*Wind up the japa with a pranaayama and a prayer to the supreme force (as you have to proceed with the worldly activities thereafter)*
Mantra 9	***Pray** and do salutations to all divine and natural forces around you - primary and secondary*
Mantra 10	*Totally surrender yourself to the divine will, that too willingly.*

Mantra 11

Pray for the good of you both in active and sleeping time by saying "please give good luck to me and my family. Please remove the ill effects of bad dreams".

Please undo the consequence / punishment for all the sins committed by me. Please grant me what is great and good.

Finish the prayer.

General: This is done sitting cross-legged or in the Padmasana pose, on a mat or wooden Palagai (a small platform) placed on the floor either in the open or inside the house. This is done facing east during prathasandhya, facing north during madyannikam and facing west during sayam sandhya.

1. Japa sankalpam™

Procedure: Recite the following mantra slowly tapping the forehead with both fists to-gether.

शुक्लांम्बरधरं विष्णुं शशिवर्णं चतुर्भुजम् ।

प्रसन्नवदनं ध्यायेत् सर्वविघ्रोप-शान्तये ॥

Shuklambaradharam Vishunum Sasi Varnam Chathur Bhujam, Prasanna Vadanam Dyayeth Sarva Vigna Upa Santhaye.

[10]The meaning and procedures are explained earlier for 1, 2 and 3.

2 Do Pranayamam

ओं भूः + भृभुवस्सुवरोम् ॥ (प्राणायामः) ॥
ओं भूःभुवः सुवः ।
ओं तत्सवितुर्वरेण्यं । भर्गोदेवस्यधीमहि ।
धियोयोनः प्रचोदयात् ॥
ओमापो-ज्योती-रसोऽमृतं-ब्रह्म
भूर्भुवस्सुवरोम् ॥

3. Keep the right palm inside the left palm and keep the palms on the right thigh and recite the following mantra.

ममोपात्त-समस्तदुरितक्षय-द्वारा
श्रीपरमेश्वरप्रीत्यर्थं
प्रातः सन्ध्या-गायत्री-महामंत्र-जपं करिष्ये ।
माध्याह्निक-गायत्री-महामंत्र-जपं करिष्ये ।
सायं सन्ध्या-गायत्री-महामंत्र-जपं करिष्ये ॥

Mamo paatha samasta durita kshaya dwaara, Sri Parameshwara Preethyartham pratas sandhya gayathri mahaa mantra

▶▶▶▶

japam karishye

(for madhyannikam instead tell)

"madhyanika gayathri mahaa mantra japam karishye" and for evening sandhya vandhanam tell "saayam sandhyaa gayathri mahaa mantra japam karishye".

4. Japam

Meaning: *Om is the first part of the Mantra.* For "Om" the Rishi is Brahma. Gayatri is the "metre". The supreme energy is the devata (the prayer is addressed to him.)

For the Seven frequencies the respective Rishis are Atri, Brugu, Kutsa, Vasistha, Gauthama, Kashyapa and Angirasa. The metres are Gayatri, Ushnik, Anushtup, Bhruhati, Pangthi, Thrushtup, Jagati.

Agni (Fire), Vayu (air) Arka (Sun), Vageesa (Brihaspathi), Varuna (varuna) Indra (Indra) and Visvedevata (all other gods) are the devatas.

Procedure: While praying -remember the Rishi in the head, metre on the tongue and the concerned "devata" in the heart.

The first is called the Pranava japam shown under 4.A. Here you focus by repeating "Om"

The second part focuses on the 7 vyahrutis or worlds. This is shown under 4B. This is done in the form of breathing exercise (Pranayama)

4. A. Pranava japam

प्रणवजपः-प्राणायामः ॥१३॥

प्रणवस्य ऋषिर्ब्रह्म, देवी-गायत्री छन्दः,

परमात्मा देवता ॥

Pranavasya Rishi Brahma
(touch the forehead with fingers),

▶▶▶▶

Devi Gayathri Chandaha
>   (touch below the nose),

Paramathma devatha
>   (touch the middle of the chest)

4. B. The second part of the Mantra is the seven frequencies cum energy bands that are generally referred to "Bhur" to "sathyam".

भूरादि-सप्त-व्याहृतीनां अत्रि-भृगु-कुत्स-

वसिष्ठ-गौतम-काश्यप-आंगिरस ऋषयः ॥

गायत्री-उष्णिक्-अनुष्टुप्-बृहती-पंक्ती-तृष्टुप्

जगती छन्दाँसि ॥ अग्नि-वायु-अर्क-वागीश-

वरुण-इन्द्र-विश्वेदेवा-देवताः ॥१३.१॥

Bhooraadhi saptha vyahrudeenaam athri -
brugu - kuthsa - vasishta - gowthama -
kaasyapa - aangeerasa rishaya
(touch fore head)
Gayathree - ushnig - anushtup - brahathi
- pankthi - trushtup - jagathi chandaamsi
(touch below the nose)
Agni - vaayu - arka - vaageesa - varuna -
indra -viswe deva - devatha
(touch the middle of the chest)

5. *Do Pranayama ten times*

Meaning: Om is emblematic of the su-preme spirit-just as images are of the material things. In other words Om is the sound repre-sentation of the universal spirit. Bhur to sathyam are seven frequency bands that covers the entire cosmos. Om has the power to cut through the seven frequencies so as to carry the messages to the supreme spirit where ever he is.

By doing 4 and 5 you are prepared to launch the message (meant for transmission).

ओं भूः । ओं भुवः । ओश़ सुवः ।
ओं महः । ओं जनः । ओं तपः ।
ओश़सत्यम् ।। ओं तत् सवितुर्वरेण्यं भर्गों
देवस्य धीमहि । धियो यो नः प्रचोदयात् ।।
ओमापो-ज्योती-रसोऽमृतं-ब्रह्म
भूर्भुवस्सुवरोम् ।।१३.२।।

6. *Gayathri avahanam*

Meaning: For the following mantra starting with the word "Aayathu", the sage is Vaama Deva, meter is Anushtup and Goddess is Gaayathri.

Gayathri mantra is the essence of Vedas. The term "Mantra" refers to the "thought". The external form of that thought - in the form of "word and metre" - is known as Gayatri. The inner life of that Mantra, which is in the form of light is known as Savitri .The knowledge and true understanding of the Mantra is referred to as Saraswati.

Here we praise and pray to that form – refered to as Gayatri as follows:

The goddess Gayathri who can give all desired boons, who is ever permanent, who is known by understanding Vedas and who is the mother of all meters should come to me. Let my prayer be granted. Oh Mother Gayathri, you are the power of the soul supporting air, you are the power of all organs, You have power to win over all enemies, You are the resplendent light, You are the brightness of all Gods, You are the universe, You are time - the soul of the universe, You are soul of everything, You are victorious over everything. You are all the above and beyond these qualities (which I can not describe). So I pray to you who is the very meaning of the word "Om".

Then we say that: I want to absorb with in me the structure of thee mantra, the power of the

Mantra and the the knowledge realting to them.

Procedure: while reciting the last three manthras, after avahayami, keep both the palms together with little fingers touching and then slowly take the finger towards oneself, and bring it back to original position after one rotation)

Mantra :

गायत्री-आवाहनम् ॥१४॥

आयात्वित्यनुवाकस्य, वामदेव ऋषिः ।

अनुष्टुप् छन्दः । गायत्री देवता ॥

आयातु वरदा देवी अक्षरं ब्रह्मसंमितम् ।

गायत्रीं छन्दसां मातेदं ब्रह्म जुषस्व नः ॥

▶▶▶▶

अीजोंऽसि सहोंऽसि बलमसि भ्राजोंऽसि
देवानां धाम नामासि विश्वमसि विश्वायुः
सर्वमसि सर्वायु-रभिभूरों (TS 2.4.3.2)
गायत्री-मावाहयामि सावित्री-मावाहयामि
सरस्वती-मावाहयामि ॥१४.१॥

Aayadithi anuvagasya vamadeva rishi
(touch head), Anushtup chandaha
(touch below nose),
Gayathri devatha
(touch the middle of the chest)
Aayathu varada devi aksharam brahma
samhitham.
Gayathrim chandasam mathedam brahma
jushaswana.
Ojosi, sahosi, balamasi, brajosi,
devaanaam dhama naamaasi.
Viswamasi, viswayu
sarvamasi, sarvayu
abhiboorom, Gayathrim aavahayami,
Savithrim aavahayami,
saraswathim aavahayami

6.7 Gayathri Nyasam[11]

For the Gayathri Manthra, the sage is Viswamithra, metre is Nichrut - Gayathri and the God is Savitha.

गायत्री-न्यासः

सावित्र्या ऋषि-विश्वामित्रः । निचृद्गायत्री छन्दः ।

सविता देवता ॥१४.२॥

Savithrya rishi Viswamitraha
        (touch the fore head),
nichrud gayathri chandaha
        (touch below the nose),
savitha devatha
        (touch the middle of the chest)

£OCS

[11]Nyasa is done to experience the Supreme power within one's gross body.

▶▶▶▶

Meditation is the focusing of the mental & intellectual energy towards the Mantra/thought. It is the art of communicating with the other forces around us and the Supreme energy. Once you focus, the mind gets access to intuitive knowledge.

GAYATRI MANTRA

Gayatri mantra is one of the most popular mantras and is interpreted in a number of ways - though all these interpretations/commentaries have the same theme and core thought.

One can follow any interpretation or meaning. But one thing is definite. When one chants one should roll over the meaning in the mind. By focusing, the mind becomes profound and peaceful. When one knows the meaning intellect will have no doubt whatsoever and meditation becomes peaceful.

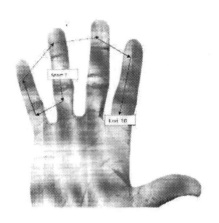

"Gayathri Mantra is chanted for the attainment of universal consciousness and for the awakening of the Intuitive powers"

▶▶▶▶

How to keep count?

1. Use a japa mala: A japa mala (made from the stem of a tulsi plant or rudraksha beeds) with 108 beeds can be used for reciting, chanting or mentally repeating the mantra

2. The counting with out japamala

- The right hand can be used to keep the count of "ones". This is done by using the segments in each finger - by pointing the thumb on the same hand. The movement has to be clockwise. Start from the middle segment in the ring finger (1,2), go up on the little finger (3,4,5), move on to the top segment of the ring, middle and index finger (6,7,8) come down on the index finger (9,10). Then start again in the same way. Use the fingers in the left hand to keep the count of "tens". The movement in the left hand is anti clockwise.

7. *Gayathri japam*

Meaning: We meditate on that resplendent form of God, who is the meaning of the word "OM", Who sharpens our intellect, and who is the creator. Let that force arouse my energy.

Savitr is not the physical sun that we see but is the supreme effulgence-the true creator of all the forces. The physical sun that we see is only taken as representative of the premordial energy.

"Diyo yona prachodhayad" is the message that we want to pass on to the Supreme Spirit.

▶▶▶▶

Procedure: Repeat 108 times the Gayathri mantra (in the morning and evening) facing east in the morning, west in the evening. 32 times at noon facing east.

Mantra:

गायत्री-जपम्

ओम् । भूर्भुवस्सुवः ।

तत्सवितुर्वरेण्यम् । भर्गो देवस्य धीमहि ।

धियो यो नः प्रचोदयात् ॥

"Om Bhorbuvaswa, tat sa vithur varenyam, bhargo devasya deemahi, dhiyo yona Prachodayaat[12]

While doing the meditation

Once you sit in a posture you should not move as the spiritual energy pervades the whole ambience. One should sit firmly. Keep the trunk, head and neck erect.

[12] RV 3.62.10, TA 4.35,SV 1462

> ### *There are five methods/techniques of doing Gayatri Japa. Follow any method that suits you.*
>
> *Vaikhari Japa* - Memorise the mantra. Say it loudly and clearly.
>
> *Upaamsu Japa:* Mutter the mantra in a very low voice - lips and tongue alone move. Mind should be on the meaning of the mantra.
>
> *Madhyama Japa:* Repeat the mantra mentally. Focus on the central meaning/theme of the mantra. Hear the mantra in the heart.
>
> *Pashyanti Japa:* Mentally reverberate the sound. Gradually with practice you will tend to see the sound vibration in colours. You see the mantra - i.e. sound and light manifesting as light. You experience visible sound.
>
> *Para Japa:* Be in perfect silence. Meditate on Om and Mantra.
>
> Start with the first method and gradually you will shift to the other method - which suits you the best. Don't get carried away by examining why you are not able to follow one particular method etc.

One way to communicate to the Supreme energy through Gayatri Mantra

Sit in a convenient place and posture.

Say OM loudly or within yourself (which ever suits you) and thereby generate a carrier wave which would take your message to that Supreme power.

Spread the carrier wave in all directions and frequencies - by saying **"Bhur Bhuva Swah"**. One should be aware of these planes in us - physical, life energy and mental. The third plane "Swah" was later classified into Suvah, Mahar, Jana and Thapa, according to their subtlety level.

Focus your mind on the Supreme energy saying "Tat savithur varenyam, bhargo devasya deemahi" and thereby load the message "dhiyo yona pracho -dayath".

Mentally communicate your

Prayer request in this way.

A thought given by SAI

Life on earth is possible only because of the Sun. For mankind that is caught up in a meaningless existence and going through an endless round of futile activities, the Sun God stands out as an exemplar of tireless and selfless service. **He enjoys no respite from work. He is above praise and censure. He carries on his duties with absolute equanimity. Everything he does is only for the wellbeing of the world and not for causing any harm. Thus the Sun God teaches us the supreme example of humble devotion to duty, without any conceit. Everyone must learn how to do their duties with devotion and dedication, just like the Sun. Doing one's duty is the greatest *Yoga* (Spiritual path), as pointed out by Krishna in the Gita.** Hence, let your actions and thoughts be good. You will then experience the bliss divine.

UPASTHANAM

This good bye is identical to the "bye" that we say at the end of a telephonic conversation in our day to day life – bye for now. The true meaning is that we get back to world of action and meet after some time.

This conversation itself demonstrates our mutual strength yet mutual dependence on the other forces in this Universe.

The concept of Upasthanam ie saying "good bye" has also a deeper significance. While it is essential to carry out a self review and mental dialogue with the Supreme power that runs this Universe, it is equally important to demonstrate those principles and the values enshrined in them practically through our action – in our day to day life.There is no substitute to action.

So also, Sandhya vandhanam is not a mere theoretical exercise or a prayer or a self examination but it is a stimulant to greater action – especially in line with the principles brought out in them. The formal closure – by saying good bye – is to bring home to the practitioner of Sandhya vandhanam to get back to the world of action.

In the real sense, it is not a good bye to the Supreme but is to formally close the practice session. So if you follow the true spirit, you will get back to world of action with greater determination and mental courage.

8. A. Gayathri Upasthanam

Gayathri Upasthana mantra alone is same for all the three sessions. However other Upasthana mantras are different for the three sessions.

Meaning:

*   I am requesting the Goddess of Morning (or evening) to go back to her place.

*   After blessing us who pray to you, please be kind enough to bless us. Go and occupy your rightful place, happily at your convenience which is on the holy peak.

Procedure:

Do pranayamam and then stand up and chant.

गायत्री-उपस्थानम्

प्राणायामः ।। प्रातः सन्ध्या, (आदित्य), (सायं सन्ध्या), उपस्थानं करिष्ये ।। उत्तमें शिखरे देवी भूम्यां पर्वत-मूर्धनि । ब्राह्मणेभ्यो ह्मनुज्ञानं गच्छ देवि यथा सुखम् ।।

Facing the same direction

Praatha sandhyaam upasthaanam karishye

(during pratha sandhya)

Adithyam upasthaanam karishye

(during madyannikam)

Sayam sandhyaupasthaanam karishye

(during sayam sandhya)

Then repeat

Uthame shikare devi, bhoomyam parvatha murdhini, Brahmanebhyo Hyanugnanam, gacha devi yada sukham.

8. B. Surya Upasthanam

For Surya Upasthanam the mantras are different for each session.

During morning (pratha sandhya)

Meaning: Mitra is associated with morning light. He is the protector of the universe during the day and hence this prayer is addressed mitra in the morning. I meditate on the greatness and fame of the Sun God who protects all people, who is truly praise worthy, who is the greatest at all times, who steals the heart and mind of everyone through his greatness. He knows everything and every happenings, he guides people. He carries the earth and the heaven. He is watching the world (perennially), without blinking his eye. To get his blessings and through that things that are best for me- I make this offering. (Filled with ghee.)

Oh Sun God! You are also known as Mithra. Whosoever worships you sincerely and devotedly become fully capable of good and great deeds. Such person is protected by you. He will never become sick or affected by any ailments. Even his misdeeds will also not trouble him. Who so ever wants to worship you become fully capable of holy deeds. He who is protected by you never becomes sick and sins will not trouble him, either from far and near.

सूर्य-उपस्थानम्

प्रातः-मित्रस्य चर्षणी धृतः
श्रवो देवस्य सानसिम् ।
सत्यं चित्रश्रवस्तमम् ॥
मित्रो जनान् यातयति प्रजानन् मित्रो
दाधार पृथिवी-मुत द्याम् ।
मित्रः कृष्टी-रनिमिषाभिचष्टे सत्याय हव्यं
घृतवद्विधेम ॥
प्र स मित्र मर्तो अस्तु प्रयस्वान् यस्त
आदित्य शिक्षति व्रतेन ।
न हन्यते न जीयते त्वोतो नैनमꣳहो
अश्नोत्यन्तितो न दूरात् [13] ॥

Mithrasya charshanee drutha sravo
devasya saanaseem,
sathyam chithra sravasthamam
Mithro janan yaatayathi prajanan mithro

[13] Ts 3.4.11

▶▶▶▶

dhaadhaara prithveem udadhyaam.
Mithra krushti ranimisha bichashte
sathyaya havyam ghrutavath vidhema
Prasa mithra martho asthu prayaswaan
yastha adithya sikshathi vratena
Na hanyathe na jeeyathe thwotho nainam
agmho asnothyantito na dooraath

During noon (madyaneekam)

The Sun is the custodian of "day". Hence this prayer is addressed to sun at noon.

Meaning:

The Sun God Who is resplendent and who travels with his visible light which makes the people of earth and heaven do their allotted duties. He travels in his golden chariot inspecting all the world. His horses, which are his rays, carry the Sun God who is well known in the Vedas and who knows everything and travel round the sky so that we the people of earth can all see him.

This refers to the Sun being the primary source of energy and being the primary form of energy for the earth.

We see the Sun God, who rises daily after swallowing darkness and who with his light protects the Devas.

The Sun God, who is like an eye to Mithra, Varuna and Agni and who is the personification of all devas, travels very high in the sky. The Sun God, who is the soul of those who are mobile and also those who are immobile, spreads throughout the heaven, earth and the atmosphere. Rising in the east and doing good to all the gods the sun is like an eye.

This refers to the Sun being at the centre of the Solar system and being seen at different angles during the Earth rotation and revolution.

Let the Sun God who gives us all boons, who has reddish eyes, who knows every thing, who shines in all directions and who rises from the middle of the vast ocean in the dawn make me holy.

We want to live long - for hundred years seeing, enjoying and benefitting from sun (his energy). Bless us with long and happy life.

मध्याह्ने- आसत्येन रजसा वर्तमानो

निवेशयन्नमृतं मर्त्यं च हिरण्ययेन सविता

रथेनाऽद्देवो याति भुर्वना विपश्यन् ॥१७॥

(T .S.3.4.1 1)

उद्वयं तमसस्परि पश्यन्तो ज्योतिरुत्तरम् ।

देवं देवत्रा सूर्यमगन्म ज्योतिरुत्तमम् ।

उदुत्यं जातवेदसं देवं वहन्ति केतवः ।

दृशे विश्वाय सूर्यै ।। (T .S.1.4.43, 1.2.9)
चित्रं देवाना-मुदगा-दनीकं
चक्षु-र्मित्रस्य वरुणस्याग्नेः ।
आ प्रा द्यावा पृथिवी अन्तरिक्ष॰
सूर्यं आत्मा जगत-स्तस्थुषश्च । (T .S.1.4.43)
तच्चक्षु-र्देवहितं पुरस्ता-च्छुक्र मुच्चरत् ।।
पश्येम शरदश्शतं, जीवेम शरदश्शतं,
नन्दाम शरदश्शतं, मोदाम शरदश्शतं,
भवाम शरदश्शतं॰ शृणवाम शरदश्शतं,
प्रब्रवाम शरदश्शत-मजीतास्याम शरदश्शतं
ज्योक् च सूर्यै दृशे ।।
य उदगान्महतोऽर्णवाद्विभ्राजमानः
सरिरस्य मध्यान् समा वृषभो लोहिताक्ष
- स्सूर्यो विपश्चिन् मनसा पुनातु[14] ।।१७.२।।

([14]TS 3.4.11, 4.3.1, 4.1.7 TA 1.4.42)

Aasathyena rajasaa varthamano
nivesayan amrutham marthyancha Hiranyena
savithaa rathena aadevo yaathi

bhuvana vipasyan Udvayam

thamasaparee pasyantho jyothiruthamam

Devam devathra soorya maganma

Jyothiruttamam Uduthyam jaata vedasam

devam vahanti ketavaha

Druse viswaya sooryai

Chitram devaana mudagaa daneekam

chakshu mithrasya varunasyagneaapraa

dyaava pruthvi aanthareeksha soorya

aatma jagathasthushaca

Tachakshur deva hitam purasthath chukra
Mucharath Pashyemah sharadas shatham,
Jeevemah sharadas shatham, Nandhaamah
sharadas shatham, Modhamah sharadas
shatham, Bhavamah sharadas shatham,
Srunuvaamah sharadas shatham,
Prabravaamah sharadas shatham,
Ajeethasyaamah sharadas shatham
Jyok cha surye dhrushe
Ya udagath mahatornavaat
Vibhraajamana salilasya madhyaath
Samah vrishabhoh lohithaksha
Suryo vipashyan manasaa punathu

During evening (Sayam sandhya)

Varuna is the custodian of "Night". Hence
this prayer is addressed to Varuna in in the
evening.

I pray to you using Veda mantras and fall at your feet.Even in yagna we give the offering to you through fire God. O famous God Varuna, without neglect, be pleased to hear my prayer. Please never reduce my life span.

Oh God Varuna, we might not have worshipped you daily due to carelessness.

Knowingly or unknowingly we men might have deceived the Devas in worship, we might have spoiled your good deeds. Oh God Varuna, please do not punish us for these sins.

We might have also been defamed without basis by bad people like gamblers.

We might have done some sins fully knowing it. We might have done a few sins without knowing it. Please destroy them in to small pieces, without causing pain to anyone. Please keep me as one who is very dear and close to you.

We will see him for hundred springs, We would live for hundred springs, We would enjoy life with all those who are dear for hundred springs, We would live with fame for hundred springs, We would hear sweet words for hundred springs, We would live without being won by bad deeds for hundred springs, Like this we wish to see our dear Sun God for a long long time.

This refers to how man indiscriminately uses different natural resources and energy and resources. Sometimes either in bad company or due to selfish interest Man might have mis-used it. We wish to correct that situation.

सायंकाले-इमं मे वरुण श्रुधी हव॑-मद्या च॑ मृडय ।
त्वाम॑वस्युरा॒च॑के ॥ तत्त्वा॑ यामि॒ ब्रह्मणा॒ वन्द॑मान-
स्तदाशा॑स्ते॒ यज॑मानो ह॒विर्भिः ॥

अहे॑डमानो वरुणे॒ह बो॒ध्युरुं॒श॒ स॒ मा॒ न॒ आयुः
प्रमो॑षीः॥ (TS 2.1.1 1, 2.1.22,21,22) यच्चि॒द्धि ते॒ विशो॑
यथा॒ प्रदे॑व वरुण व्रतम् । मि॒नी॒मसि॒ द्यवि॑ द्यवि ॥

यत्किं चे॒दं व॑रुण॒दैव्ये॒ जने॑ऽभिद्रो॒हं म॑नुष्या॒श्चर॑मसि ।
अचि॒त्तीयत्त॑व॒ धर्मा॑ युयोपिम मा न॑स्तस्मादेन॑सो
देव रीरिषः । कि॒त॒वासो॒ यद्रि॑रिपुर्-न॑दीवि यद्वा॒घा
सत्य॑-मु॒तयन्न॒ विद्म । सर्वा॒ ता वि॒ष्य॑ शिथि॒रेव॑
दे॒वाथा॒ ते स्याम वरुण प्रि॒यासः ॥१७.३॥

Sayamkale

Imam me varuna sruthi hava madhyaa cha mrudaya

thvaam mavsyu rachake

tathwayaami brahmana vandamanas

thadhaasaasthe yajamano havirbhi

Ahedamano varuneha bhodyurusaghum samaa na aayu pramoshi

yacchidithe visho yadha pradheva varuna vratham miniimasi dyavi dyavi

yat kinchedam varuna daivye janeabhi droham manushyaas charamasi

Achithee yath thavaa dharma yuyopimaa

Maanasthasmath enaso deva reerishaha

Kitha vaso yadri ripur nadheevi yad vagha duscharitham mamah

sathya muthayanna vidhma

sarvaa thaa vishya sithireva devathaa the syaama varuna priyasaha

9. Samashti Abhivadanam

9.1. *Meaning:* My salutations to Sandhya, Savitri, Gayatri and Saraswati (located in different directions).

▶▶▶▶

Procedure: Starting from the direction facing which the japa was done, turn 90 degrees after each mantra, to the right. Say the next manthra and so on.

समष्ट्यभिवादनम्

सन्ध्यायै नमः । सावित्र्यै नमः । गायत्र्यै नमः । सरस्वत्यै नमः ।

Sandhyaayai namaha   Saavithryai namaha

Gaaythryai namaha   Saraswatyai namaha

9.2. ***Meaning:*** My salutations to all devatas.

Procedure: Then chant with folded hands facing the same direction.

सर्वाभ्यो देवताभ्यो नमो नमः ॥

Sarvaabhyo devathabhyo namo nama

9.3. *Meaning:* Anger and selfish desire made me err. I acted under their bad influence. Please protect me from them. I did not do it willingly.

Procedure: Then chant facing the same direction.

कामोऽकार्षीन्मन्युरकार्षीन्नमो नमः ।।

Kamo karsheen manyura karsheen namo namaha.

9.4. Meaning:

Abhivadaye (I present my self)

(Tell the names of rishis, whose descendents are your family- Tell number of such Rishis) Risheya

(Tell the name of the (pravara) founder of your clan) pravaranvitha (tell your Gothra/Clan) gothra (tell your Suthra- the Law code you follow)suthraha (Tell your Veda/way of life you plan to follow) shaaka adhyaaye Sri (tell your name) sarmanam aham asmibhoho

This information (gothra and pravaraa) has to be obtained from elderly members of your family.

Then touch with both hands the ears slightly bow and chant. (Abivadanam) After this touch your feet with both hands and do namaskaram.

This is your formal introduction to your community:

अभिवादये (वैश्वामित्र,आघमर्षण, कौशिक, त्रय)
आर्षेय प्रवरान्वित, (कौशिक) गोत्र:,
(आपस्तंब) सूत्र:, (यजु:) शाखाध्यायी,
श्री(कृष्ण) शर्मा नामाहं अस्मि भो: ॥

Special Prayers :

The Gayatri Japa and the Upasthana mantras are followed by a set of prayers eulogizing the Various other forces that run this Universe.

There are over 330 million types of energy forms (devatas) that run this universe. Each energy (devata) operates at different but discrete frequencies. Each and every energy contributes to our living - in some way or the other. The mind has to link to those energies to get the needed strength. The devata vandhanam onwards is an effort towards that linking. The following portion varies slightly for different people, though the spirit of worship remain the same.

9.5 Dig devatha vandhanam

Meaning: My salutations to the Protectors of each direction/side.

Salutations to the	East
Salutations to the	South
Salutations to the	West
Salutations to the	North
Salutations to the	Gods above
Salutations to the	Gods below
Salutations to the	Atmosphere
Salutations to the	Earth
Salutations to the	Brahma
Salutations to the	Vishnu
Salutations to the	God of death

Procedure:

With folded hands offer salutations to the different directions facing that direction:

दिग्देवता-वन्दनम् ।।
प्राच्यै दिशे नम । दक्षिणायै: दिशे नम :
प्रतीच्यै दिशे नमः । उदीच्यै दिशे नमः ।।

▶▶▶▶

ऊर्ध्वाय नमः । अधराय नमः ।
अन्तरिक्षाय नमः । भूम्यै नमः ।
ब्रह्मणे नमः । विष्णवे नमः ।
मृत्यवे नमः ।।

Pracyai dishe nama	(east)
Dakshinayai dishe nama	(south)
Pradeechai dishe nama	(west)
Udichyai dishe nama	(north)

Then again face the direction in which you did japa and continue.

Oordwaaya nama	(above)
Adharaaya nama	(below)
Anthareekshaaya nama	(straight)
Bhoomyai nama	(earth)
Brahmane nama	
Vishnave nama	
Mrutuyuve nama	

========

9.6. Yama Vandanam

Meaning: My salutations to yama.

- You control every thing.

- you ensure that every dharma is followed

- you are the destroyer of every thing by bringing death.

- you are the progeny of Vivaswan

- you are the controller of time

- you are the destroyer of all animals

- you are a very strong man.

- you are known as Dhadnan

- you are dark in complexion

- you are worshipped by every body

- you are the protector and keeper of strange secrets relating to life.

Procedure: Turn towards south and offer this prayer.

▶▶▶▶

यमवन्दनम् ।।

यमाय नमः ।

यमाय धर्मराजाय मृत्यवे चान्तकाय च ।

वैवस्वताय कालाय सर्वभूत-क्षयाय च ।।

औदुंबराय दघ्नाय नीलाय परमेष्ठिने ।

वृकोदराय चित्राय चित्रगुप्ताय वै नमः ।।

चित्रगुप्ताय वै नम ओं नम इति ।।

Yamaya namah

Yamaya dharma rajaya, mrutyuve cha anthakaaya ca

Vaivaswataaya kalaaya sarva bhoota kshayaayacha

Oudhumbharaaya dhagnaya neelaaya parameshtine

Vrukodharaya chithraaya chithra guptaaya vai namah

Chithra gupthaya vai nama om nama iti

9.7. Harihara Vandhanam

Meaning: This is addressed to "Rta" - meaning the law of this cosmic world. In effect rta denotes the order of the world. The whole universe is founded on rta and moves in it. We bow before that order.

You are the beauty of the cosmic order, worldly truths, the real supreme power, you assume all the forms of Shiva, Vishnu and Brahma. My salutations to you.

Rta is important as it gives "faith on tomorrow". This reaffirms to us that the universe is not a chaos but is working harmoniously. It is this faith on tomorrow that keeps the world forward looking and progressive. Hence this prayer is directed towards that order.

Procedure : Turn towards North and offer this prayer.

हरिहरवन्दनम् ॥

ऋतꣳ सत्यं परं ब्रह्म पुरुषं कृष्ण-पिंगलम् ।

ऊर्ध्वरेतं विरूपाक्षं विश्वरूपाय वै नमः ।

विश्वरूपाय वै नम ओन्नम इति ॥

Ruthagum sathyam para brahma purusham

Krishna pingalam

Oordhwretam viroopaksham

Viswa roopaaya vai namah

Viswa roopaya vai nama om nama ithi

9.8. Soorya Narayana Vandhanam

Meaning : My salutations to Savitr-who is seen as Lord Surya Narayana, who is like an eye to the universe, Who is the cause of birth, upkeep and destruction of the worlds, Who is personification of Vedas and Who by his three qualities takes the form of the holy trinity of Brahma, Vishnu and Shiva,

Lord Narayana is forever most suitable to be venerated for he is the middle of the solar system, For he sits in the lotus pose, For he wears the crown on the head, chain on his neck, wears anklets in his Arms and wears studs in his ears, For he holds the Conch and the wheel in his hands and has the glittering colour of gold.

Oh Lord who holds the conch and wheel in his hand, who forever lives in Dwaraka, Who takes care of all beings of the earth and Who has lotus like eyes, please protect me who has come and fallen at your feet.

Like all the water that falls from the sky reaches the sea, all salutations done to all gods reach Lord Narayana.

▶▶▶▶

सूर्यनारायणवन्दनम् ॥

नमःसवित्रे जगदेक-चक्षुषे जगत्-प्रसूति-स्थिति-नाश

- हेतवे । त्रयी-मयाय त्रिगुणात्म-धारिणे विरिंचि -
नारायण-शंकरात्मने ॥

ध्येयः सदा सवितृमण्डल - मध्यवर्ती नारायणः
सरसिजासन-संनिविष्टः । केयूर-वान्
मकरकुण्डलवान्
किरीटी हारी हिरण्मयवपु-धृत-शंख-चक्रः ॥

शंख-चक्र-गदापाणे द्वारकानिलयाच्युत ।
गोविन्द पृण्डरीकाक्ष रक्ष मां शरणागतम् ॥

आकाशात् पतितं तोयं यता गच्छति सागरम् ।
सर्वदेव-नमस्कारः श्रीकेशवं प्रति गच्छति ॥

श्रीकेशवं प्रति गच्छत्यों नम इति ॥

अभिवादये+अस्मि भोः ॥ (नमस्कारः) ॥

Nama savithre jagadeka chakshushe, Jagat
prasoothi sthithi naasa hethave, Trayin mayaya
trigunathma dharine

Virinchi Narayana sankara athmane

Dyeya sada savithru mandala Madhya varthi

Narayana sarasijasana sannivishta

Keyuravan makara kundalavaan

Kiriti haari hiranya vapur drutha sankha
chakra

Sanka chakra gatha pane dwaraka
nilayachythe

Govinda pundarikaksha raksha

maam sarana gatham

Aakasath pathitham

thoyam Yathaa gachathi sagaram

Sarva deva namaskara

Sri kesavam prathi gachathi

Sri kesavam prathi gachathi om na ithi

9.9. Prayer for protection from Snakes

Some families face the north after this and chant the following Sarpa Raksha

Meaning: This is a prayer which some of the families only follow. The first part is a prayer to the River Narmada . May be, some of

▶▶▶▶

our ancestors lived on the banks of Narmada, before migrating to other places.The second part is directed towards serpents. This mantra is also known as "Sarpa Raksha Mantra". It is believed that some planetary positions at ones birth can cause set backs in life and create obstacles in some ways. To get rid of such negative effects this mantra is included in the daily prayer itself - in some families.

When Janamejaya did a sarpa yaga to massacre of serpents, it was stopped at the intervention of Saint Astika. This mantra recalls that incident and seeks reciprocation from the serpents in our life - by not disturbing us in our day to day life. The prayer seeks their support for us.

The serpents may also represent the different worldly activities that distract us from our focus. We need not kill these distractions since they serve a purpose, but we can be conscious of it, so that they do not disturb our activities.

Manthram:

नर्मदायै नमः प्रातः नर्मदायै नमो निशि ।
नमोस्तु नर्मदे तुभ्यं त्राहि मं विष सर्पतः ।।

Narmadayai Nama -Prathar
narmadayai namo nisi Namosthu
narmadhe thubhyam trahi maam
visha sarpatha

अप सर्प सर्प बद्रम् ते दूरं गच्छ महायशाः ।
जनमेजयस्य यज्ञान्ते अस्तीक वचनम् स्मरन् ।
जरतकारोः जरतकार्वां समुत्पन्न महायशाः ।
अस्तीक सत्यसन्दोमां पन्नकेभ्यो अभिरक्षतु ।।

Apa sarpa sarpa bhadram the Dooram gacha
maha yasa Janamejayasya yagnanthe aasthika
vachanam smaran Jarath karer Jarath karvam
samuthpanno   maha yasa Aasthika Sathya
santho maam pannagebhyo abhi rakshathu.
Then do sashtanga pranamam after reciting
Abhivadaye as explained above.

========

▶▶▶▶

10. Samarpanam:

Meaning : I give away To the Lord Narayana, all the actions done by me either by my body, or by my words, or by my mind, or by my organs, or my mind or by my intellect or by my soul or by my superior thought process or by my natural movements.

In some moments in life, we wonder whether we are taking up the right actions. In such situations, if we surrender all actions to a bigger cosmic force, we will feel secure. Hence you surrender.

Procedure: Take a small quantity of water recite the following manthra and pour it on the ground.

समर्पणम् ।।

कायेन वाचा मनसेन्द्रियैर्वा, बुद्ध्यात्मना वा
प्रकृतेः स्वभावात् । करोमि यद्यत् सकलं
परस्मै नारायणायेति समर्पयामि ।। (आचमनम्) ।।

Kaayena vaacha manase indriyair vaa
Budhyathma naava prakrutai swabhavat
Karomi yadyat sakalam parasmai
Naaraayana yeti samarpayaami
Then do aachamanam

11. Raksha

Meaning: Hey Lord Savitha (Sun), please grant good luck to me and my family. Please remove the ill effects of bad dreams. Please take away remove the punishments for the sins committed by me. And please grant me what is great and good.

Procedure: Sprinkle some water on the place where japa was performed reciting the manthra below, then touch the ground with ring finger and place it between the eyelids.

=========

▶▶▶▶

रक्षा ॥

अ॒द्या नो॑ देवसवितः प्र॒जाव॑त् साव॒ीः सौ॑भगम् ।
प॒रा दुःष्वप्न्यँ॑ सुव ॥

विश्वा॑नि देव सवित॒र्दुरि॒तानि॒ प॒रा सुव ।
य॒द्भ॒द्रं तन्म॒ आ॑सुव ॥

इति सन्ध्यावन्दन-उत्तरभागः ॥

Adhya no deva savitha praja vath
saavee soubhagam para duswapneeya
suva Viswani deva savitha -durithani
paraa suvaa Yad bhadram thama
asuva

==========

VII Samithadhana

Why samitadhana?   There is no substitute to "action" while we are in this world; Mere strength and a good mind alone are not good enough. One needs an aspiration to work, perform and achieve in this world. While chapters V ans VI, focused on the basic necessities of life - namely a good, trained mind– Chapter VII focuses on realizing the needed aspiration and "will" to perform. Agni is the symbol of aspiration and will. Sun is the kindler of that aspiration in the minds and hearts of human beings/plants and animals.

Hence this section is focused on Agni and Sun. This is structured in the form of offerings to Agni. The offering is the banyan twigs/palasa tree twigs - commonly known as "samith". You offer samith as an offering (dhana) and hence the name samithadhana for this prayer.

There is a belief that Samitadhana can be performed only bachelors. The content and the spirit of these mantras do not preclude others from reciting it mentally and thereby drawing the benefits. However other methods of daily rituals are prescribed for married ones – which in spirit cover similar contents of Samidhadhanam direct or indirect.

Immediate Benefits

The positive vibrations of the Mantras energises you instantly.

Burning of peepal twigs purifies your ambience. The atmospheric pollution is reduced.

Energy can be used in two ways. Fire can be used to cook, and also to burn and therby harm. When one does not know how to use it correctly, one is under the fear of being affected by its negative aspects. Hence this act of pleasing is done.

This prayer is addressed to ''Fire'' at that point of time, about 2500 years ago. Fire was harnessed as the only source of energy, to carry out all the activities. In the modern world , you can pray to any form of energy, including atomic energy, electronic or electrical energy, etc. These Prayers are to ensure that one uses and gets the benefits of the positive and beneficial aspects of energy and at the same time is protected from its negative effects.

Meaning:

Part 1: Prayer to make me perform this offering. Praanayama and sankalpa are the same as in 1, 2, 3 and 4 under chapter V.

Part 2: Prayer: O Agni! I clean the place around you and worship you. By this practice (of this offering) I should get long life, wealth, good children. I also become a courageous person, knowledgeable, a good master, intelligent and well read among the fellow students or peers.

Part 3: Offerings: Offerings are made at the end of each of the following 13 mantras.

1. O Agni who is also known as Jathavedas, I have collected and am offering to you this samith. Just as you are bright with the burning

of samith, *you kindle the life and make it worthy - with long life, strength, food, intelligence, good personality, progeny, cattle etc.*

2. You are growing (with the burning of the sticks), so also **help us to grow.**

3. You are glittering, so also **make us glitter.**

4. You are powerful, so also **make us powerful.**

5. I am offering this. You give me the devotion and knowledge. I should get the **aura due to good personality and knowledge.**

6. Bless me **with knowledge, good children and wealth.**

7. The **various energy forces** (devas) should also know about this offering and they should bless me accordingly. (Through you, it should reach others as well).

8. I am **offering you,** who is pervading both sky and earth.

9. This **offering is to sky and earth** - the universe around us.

▶▶▶▶

10.   With the samith that I offer you should glow and because of that *I should also glow - arising out of comprehensive growth.*

11. You *protect me from* those having *an   evil eye on me (negative forces).* You make them unworthy of getting good things.

12.   With this prayer let me become a person who has *fulfilled all prayers.*

13.   One offering (without saying anything).

Part 4:   Good bye:

O Agni! Good bye to you.

Part 5: My request:

♦   With your light, let me become also a bright person.

♦   With your internal beauty let me also become beautiful internally.

♦   With your power to attract let me also become attractive and adorable.

♦   Agni! Bless me with intelligence, good
    children, O Indra! Bless me with good
    limbs and associated power.

♦   O Sun! Bless me and make me
    intelligent and a glowing personality.

> *Havan is the term for a sacred purifying
> ritual in Hinduism that involves a fire
> ceremony. It is a ritual of sacrifice made to
> the fire god Agni. If there are any spirits
> that are evil around you or even inside you
> they get burned off in the sacred fire. It is
> believed that this sacrifice will bring
> health, happiness, luck and prosperity.*

Part 6:
Seeking Pardon for shortcomings:

While doing this prayer if there were any shortcomings - in the offering, action, rendering or devotion - you condone me and accept this as a full prayer.

I realize that remembering you (The divine power) and keeping you in my thoughts is the best form of seeking pardon, prayer, penance! Hence I am doing that.

Part 7:

Protect and bless me to face and be in the world:

♦ Protect my children, off springs, cows (cattle), horses. Protect our army and warriors. I pray with this Havis.

♦ I am applying this havis as a protection on my forehead, right and left shoulders, my back, chest, neck, navel and my head.

♦ Bless me with devotion, understading, Intelligence, fame, knowledge, good mind, education, wealth, strength, long life, an aura in the personality and good health. Bless me with higher faculties/things in life!

Procedure:

Set up a small fire with coal, twigs or in any other available manner - on a small iron base. Sit in padhmaasan and start with Part 1 and 2.

Pray with folded hands Part 3.

Do parishechanam (no mantra for this) Start part.

4. Keep one samith in fire after each of the 13 mantras.

Do parishechanam (no mantra for this).

With folded hands - in standing posture -say Part 5 and 6.

Do Abhivadaya and namaskar

Take a small quantity of the ash from the havan and make a paste and apply in the respective places while saying Part 7.

। समिदाधानम् ॥

Part I

शुक्लां बरधरं+प्रीत्यर्थं प्रातस्समिदाधानं
(सायं समिदाधानं) करिष्ये ॥
लौकिकाग्निं प्रतिष्ठाप्य । अग्निमिध्वा । प्रज्वाल्य ॥

Part II

परि॒त्वाग्ने॒ परि॑मृजाम्यायुषा च॒ ध॒नेन च ।
सु प्र॒जाः प्रज॒या॑ भूयासम् । सुवीरो॑ वी॒रैस्सुव॒र्चा॑
वर्च॑सा सुपोष॒ः पोषै॑-स्सुगृ॒हो गृहै॑-प्सुपतिः पत्या॑
सुमे॒धा मे॒धया॑ सुब्रह्मा॑ ब्रह्मचा॒रि॒भिः । इत्यग्निं॑
परि॑षिच्य ॥२॥

Part III

अथ समिध-मादधाति ।

1. अ॒ग्रयै॑ स॒मिध-माहा॒र्कषं बृ॒हते जा॒तवेदसे ।
यथा॒ त्वम॑ग्ने स॒मिधा॑ समि॒ध्यस

▶▶▶▶

मामायुष॒ वर्च॑सा स॒न्यामेध॒यॉं प्र॒जया॑
पशुभि॑-र्ब्रह्मवर्च॑-सेना॒न्नाद्येन॑ सम॑ेधय॒ स्वाहा॒
॥३.१॥

2. एधॉ᳘स्येधिषी॒महि॒ स्वाहा॒ ॥३.२ ॥

3. स॒ एध॒मिद॑सि समेधिषी॒महि॒ स्वाहा॒ ॥३.३॥

4. तेजो॑ऽसि॒ तेजो॒ मयि॑ धेहि॒ स्वाहा॒ ॥३.४॥

5. अपो॑ अ॒द्यान्व॑चारिष॒ ᳘ रसे॑न॒ सम॑सृक्ष्महि ।
पय॒स्वा᳘ अ॒ग्न आग॑मं॒ तस्मा॒
स॒ ᳘ सृ॒ज वर्च॑सा॒ स्वाहा॒ ॥३.५॥

6. सं॒मा॒ग्ने॒ वर्च॑सा सृज प्र॒जया॑ च॒
धने॑न च॒ स्वाहा॒ ॥३.६॥

7. विद्युन्मे॑ अस्य॒ देवा॒ इन्द्रो॒
विद्धात्॒ सह॒ऋषि॑भिःस्वाहा॒ ॥३.७॥

8. अ॒ग्नये॑ बृ॒हते॒ नाका॑य॒ स्वाहा॒ ॥३.८॥

9. द्यावा॑-पृथि॒वीभ्या॒ ᳘ स्वाहा॒ ॥३.९॥

१०. एषा ते अग्ने समित्तया वर्धस्व
चाप्यायस्व च तयाहं वर्धमानो
भूयास-माप्यायमानश्च स्वाहा ॥३.१०॥

११. यो माग्ने भागिनᳵ सन्त-मथाभागं चिकीर्षति
।
अभागमग्ने तं कुरु मामग्ने
भागिनं कुरु स्वाहा ॥३.११॥

१२. समिध-माधायाग्ने सर्वव्रतो
भूयासᳵस्वाहा ॥३.१२॥

१३ .अथ तूष्णीं समन्तं परिषिच्य । स्वाहा ॥३.१२॥

ध्ळी ꣹

उपस्थानं करिष्ये ।

यत्ते अग्ने तेजस्तेनाहं तेजस्वी भूयासम् ।
यत्ते अग्ने वर्चस्तेनाहं वर्चस्वी भूयासम् ।
यत्ते अग्ने हरस्तेनाहं हरस्वी भूयासम् ॥ ४.१ ॥
(ᳲ ३.५.४.१४)(TS 3.5.4.14)

▶▶▶▶

Part V

मयि मेधां मयि प्रजां मय्यग्नि-स्तेजौ दधातु ।

मयि मेधां मयि प्रजां मयीन्द्र इन्द्रियं दधातु ।

मयि मेधां मयि प्रजां मयि सूर्यो भ्राजो दधातु

॥४.२॥

Part VI

अग्नये नमः । मन्त्रहीनं

क्रियाहीनं भक्तिहीनं हुताशन ।

यद्धुतं तु मया देव परिपूर्णं तदस्तु ते ॥

प्रायश्चित्तान्यशेषाणि तपः कर्मात्मकानि वै ।

यानितेषा-मशेषाणां कृष्णानुस्मरणं परम् ।

अभिवाद्य ॥४.३॥

Part VII

होम-भस्म संगृह्य । वामकरतले निधाय । अद्भिः

सेचयित्वा ॥ मानस्तोके तनये मा न आयुषि

मा नो गोषु मा नो अश्वेषु रीरिषः ।

गिरान्मानो रुद्र भामितो
वंधी-ईविष्मन्तो नर्मसा विधेम ते ।। (प्न ३.४.१
१)

मेधावी भूयासम् (ललाटे) । तेजस्वी भूयासम्
(दक्षिणबाहौ) । वर्चस्वी भूयासम् (सव्येबाहौ) ।
ब्रह्मवर्चसी भूयासम् (हृदये) । आयुष्मान्
भूयासम् (कण्ठे) । अन्नादो भूयासम् (नाभौ) ।
स्वस्ति भूयासम् (शिरसि) ।।५.१।।

श्रद्धां मेधां यशः प्रज्ञां विद्यां बुद्धिं श्रियं बलम् ।
आयुष्यं तेज आरोग्यं देहि मे हव्यवाहन ।
श्रियं देहि मे हव्यवाहन ओं नम इति ।।५.२।।

।। इति समिदाधानम् ।।

===============

Samitadhanam

Part I

(similar to Dhyanam in Sandhyavandhanam)

Shukhalaambharadharam   vishnum sasivarnam chaturbhujam
Prasanna   vadhanam   dhyaayeth   sarva vighna Upasaanthaye

(Pranayamam)
Bhu .... dhiyo yona prachodhayat

(sankalpa)
Mamopaattha samasta durita Kshayadhwaara
Sriparameswara   preethyartham
Praata (saayam in the evening) samithaadaanam karishye

Part II

Parithwaghne parivrajami aayusha
cha dhanene cha
Suprajaaha prajayaa bhuyaasam Suviroh
viiraihi suvarcha varchasaa Suposha poshaih
sugruho gruhaihi Supathibhi patya sumedha
medhaya Subrahma brahmachaaribhuhi

============

Part III

Take samidh and put in fire when you say swaahaha - every time

1.   Aghnaye samidhamahaarusham
     Brhuhate jhaata vedase
     Yathaa twam aghne samidhaa samidhyase
     Evam maam aayushaa varchasaa sanyaa
     medhayaa prajayaa pasubhir Brahma
     varchesena annadhyena Samedhaya
     swaahaha

2.   Edhosi edhishi mahi swahaaha

3.   Samidhasi samedhishi mahi swaahaaha

4.   Tejosi tejo mayi dehi swaahaaha

▶▶▶▶

5. Apoh adhyaa anvacharisham rasena sama srikshmahi payaswaan agna aagamamam thamm aasraghum shrijah varchasa swaahaaha

6. Sammaghne varchasa shrija prajaya ca dhanena ca swahaha

7. Vidhyunmeh asya dewaha indrho vidhyath saharishibhis swahaha

8. Agnaye bhruhate naakaaya swahaha

9. Dhyawa pruthwibhyam swahaha

10. Asha they aghne samiththya vardhaswa chaa aapyaayaswacha
thayaham vardhamanascha swahaha

11. Yomaaghne bhaghinaghum Santham athaa bhagham chikhirishathi Abhaghamaghne tham kuru maam aghne bhaghinam kuru swaahaaha

12. Samidham aadhayaghne sarwa vrathaha Bhuyasam swahaha

13. Swahaha (just keep the samidh on fire)

Part IV

Upasthaanam kharishye

Yette aghne thejasthenaa aham thejaswi
bhuyasam
Yette aghne varchsathenaa aham varchswi
bhuyasam
Yette aghne harasthena aham haraswi bhuyasam

Part V

Mayi medhaam mayi prajaam mai aghnihi thejoh
dadhaathu
Mayi   medhaam   mayi   prajaam   mai
indra
indhriyam dhadhathu
Mayi medhaam mayi prajaam mai suryo brahjoh
dadhaathu

Part V

Aghnaye namah
Mantra heenam kriya heenam
Bhakthi heenam huthasanaa

Yadh   hudhanthu   maya   devah
paripurnam tadasthuthe

Praayaschittaani aseshaani thapah karmaatma
kaani ca

Yaani   teshaam   aseshaanaam   sri
krishana   anusmaranam param

Say abhivadhya in full

Part VI

Take a small amount of the burnt material in your right hand, put a drop of water and make into a paste saying the following.

Maanasthoke thaneye maana aayushi maano ghoshu maano asweshu reerishaha

Veeraan mano rudra bhamito Havii avishmanto namasaa vidhemate

Apply a little paste on:

Medhaavi bhuyaasam   (face)

Tejaswi bhuyaasam   (right shoulder)

Varchaswi bhuyaasam	(left shoulder)
Brahma varcasi bhuyaasam	(chest)
Aayushmaan bhuyaasam	(neck)
Annadhou bhuyaasam	(navel)
Swasthi bhuyaasam	(navel)

Say with folded hands the following:

Shradham, medhaam, yashah, praghyaam, vidhyaam, budhim, shriyam, bhalam

Aayushyam thejah aaroghyam dhehi meh havyavahana

dhehi meh havyavahana Om namah ithi

pray and end.

VIII Prana AgniHotra

Every action one does in day to day life, he is not the only actor. The cosmic energy plays a major part. So what ever action one does he should recognise the role of this cosmic power. Take the case of a plant. One may sow a healthy seed, use good soil, nutrients and water the same regularly. Inspite of Identical situation only a few seeds come up with a leaf! The seeds need the stimulation from that cosmic energy to spring up as a plant. Similarly in every activity, the role of cosmic force can be easily traced. For example in growing food, cooking food, eating, digesting, assimilating and the very food itself.

That is why before eating the following prayer and practice are adopted.

Food is a vital for our living. While eating we say the following.

Meaning:

The divine spirit! Be kind to us.

I will follow the worldly truth and discipline along with the cosmic order and love. (Sprinkle water on food) This means we would use our energy derived by this eating to follow both the cosmic order and the worldly truth.

Let water from the base/lower layer. (Drink small quantity of water)

We are offering the food as an offering to the various constituents of the Vital Air (Prana). Let the divine power with in me derive happiness from that Supreme power/happiness.

Let water be the top layer. (Drink small quantity of water)

।। प्राणाग्नि-होत्रम् ।।

<u>Before taking the food</u>.
ओं भूर्भुवस्सुवः ।।१।।
ओं भूर्भुवस्सुवः । तत्सवितुर्वरेण्यं ।
भर्गो देवस्य धीमहि ।
धियो यो नः प्रचोदयात् ।।२।।
देव सवितः प्रसुव ।।३।।

सत्यं त्वर्तेन परिषिंचामि ।।४।।

अमृतोपस्तरण-मसि ।।५।।

प्राणाय स्वाहा । अपानाय स्वाहा ।

व्यानाय स्वाहा ।

उदानाय स्वाहा । समानाय स्वाहा ।

ब्रह्मणे स्वाहा ।।६।।

ब्रह्मणि म आत्माऽमृतत्वाय ।।७।।

After eating food
अमृतापिधान-मसि ।।८।।

।। इति प्राणाग्निहोत्रः समाप्तः।।

Prana Agnihotram

To be done before taking food

Om Bhur bhuva swah Thath
Savitr varenyam Bhargaha
devasya dhimahi Dhiyo yonah
prachodhayaat

Deva Savithaha prasuvah
Satyam thwa rthena parishinchami

Amrutha upas tahranamasi

Praanaaya swaahaaha
Apaanaaya swaahaaha
Udhaanaaya swaahaaha
Samaanaaya swaahaaha
Brahmane swahaaha
Brahmanima aatmaa amru thathwaaya

To be done after taking food
Amrutha abhidhanam asi

======

8.2 ।। यज्ञोपवीत-धारण-मन्त्रः ।।

आचम्य ।।१।।

शुक्लांबरधरं....शाान्तये ।।२।।

प्राणानायम्य ।। ओं भू....भूर्भुवस्सुवरोम् ।।

ममोपात्त-ममस्त-दुरितक्षयद्वारा श्रीपरमेश्वरप्रीत्यर्थे,
श्रौत-स्मार्त-विहित-नित्यकर्मानुष्ठान-योग्यता-
सिद्ध्यर्थं, ब्रह्मतेजोऽभिवृद्ध्यर्थे यज्ञोपवीतधारणं
करिष्ये ।।४।।

यज्ञोपवीतं इति महामन्त्रस्य । परब्रह्म ऋषिः ।
त्रिष्टुप छन्दः । परमात्मा देवता । यज्ञोपवीतधारणे
विनियोगः ।।५।।

यज्ञोपवीतं परमं पवित्रं प्रजापते-र्यत्सहजं पुरस्तात् ।
आयुष्यमग्र्यं प्रतिमुंच शुभ्रं यज्ञोपवीतं बलमस्तु
तेजः ।।६।।

आचम्य ।।७।।

उपवीतं भिन्नतन्तुं जीर्णे कश्मलदूषितं । विसृजामि
पूनर्ब्रह्मन् वर्चो दीर्घायुरस्तु मे ॥८॥

॥ इति यज्ञोपवीत-धारण-मन्त्रः समाप्तः ॥

Yagyapavitha Dharana Mantra

Do achamanam as shown in 5.1
Say the dhyana mantra as in 5.2
Do pranayaamam as per 5.3

Sankalpam :

mamo paththa samastha dhuritha kshayadwara
sri parameswara prithyartham
sroutha smartha vihitha nithya karma
anushtaana sidhyartham
brahma thejaha abhivridhyartham
yagyopavitha dharanam karishye

Yagyopavitham ithi asya mantrasya

Parabrahma rishihi

Thrushtup chandaha

Paramaatma devatha

<u>Wear the yagyopavitham - saying the
following mantra</u>

Yagyopavitham paramam pavithram
prajapathehe yatsahajam purasthaath
Aaayushyam agryam pratimuncha shubhram
Yagno pavitham balamastu tejaha

Perform achamanam as per 5.1

Remove the old poonal - saying the following mantra

If you are replacing the old poonal with a new
one –the new one is first worn and then only the old
one is removed. While removing the old one, the
following mantra is said.

Upaveetam Bhinna thanthum
jeernam kasmala dooshitham
Visrujaami punah Brahman varcho
dheergayu asthu mey.

End with Achamana as per 5.1

Meaning: I am discarding in water this
sacred thread - which has its strands broken
and which is decayed. May the radiance of
that Supreme spirit and long life be mine

On its universality

▶▶▶▶

IX. Food for Thought

A few practical suggestions are given below - to the persons who want to practice and implement this commitment to Nature and through Nature to the Supreme Energy.

Anyone who has understood the meaning of Sandhyavandanam mantras would vouch for the universality of the mantras - irrespective of the caste, creed and gender. Then why is that kept as a private property of a few selected people that too - male? Do we ever say that a particular principle of physics or an economic theory is exclusively for boys and not for girl students or vice versa? In the modern world of free interaction and equal participation in all activities by both genders, this concept of "restricted reading and practice" is not even conceivable. Is it not true that the commitment brought out in Sandhyavandanam is to be read, understood and practiced by both male and female?

b) The contents of the Sandhyavandhanam and its format makes it a complete prayer. That alone would suffice and no one need to necessarily do other forms of worship. In a way Sandhyavandhanam is like a "thali menu" served in Hotels/restaurants in India. There is no need to supplement the thali with ala - carte menu. Do you agree that the practice of Sandhyavandhanam is adequate to confirm and show our commitment to the fellow beings and natural forces?

c) A common excuse that one offers for not practicing Sandhyavandanam - is due to "lack of time". It is strange that while we all spend hours on mundane communication on mobile, social media of all types - we find no time to ensure harmonious living in this world! I think there could be a way out for the ones who are too busy in other activities. Practice Chapter V at least every day in the morning and evening. Practice Chapter VI at least on weekends -when you have relatively more time at your disposal. Do Chapter VII at least once a month - say

▶▶▶▶

first Sunday of every month (or say on all full moon days). By saying this, the intention is not to cross the rules laid down by elders in the past. But this is given as an alternative to serve as a via media to suit the modern young generation. Don't you think that the above suggested alternatives will make more and more youngsters to follow, understand and benefit from these practices?

d) Even if one cannot do the procedural part (due to various reasons) one must recite the mantras and roll over the thought in the mind with full concentration - every morning and evening. This process will also bring in the desired results.

e) No doubt the prescribed methodology specifies a few mantras to be repeated a number of time - for example 10 times, 108 times etc. Start with at least a few times that suits you -but with 100% devotion and concentration. Gradually you will automatically increase the numbers having sensed the benefits arising out of this practice.

X. A fervent Appeal to commit

In our day to day life, there is nothing like a mere worldly activity or a spiritual activity. All worldly activities are spiritual if they are done keeping the welfare of the fellow beings and Nature around us in our mind. So also, all spiritual activities will invariably lead us to a healthy and happy life - in one way or the other. We partner with Nature in this effort. This is the basic truth realised and expounded by Hindu thinkers. The need is only to realise, train and tune our mind to this principle. Sandhya vandanam is a formal practice towards this end. This practice of Sandhyavandanam prepares and reenergises one's mind to contribute towards - a green world and a healthy and happy society - around us.

▶▶▶▶

To conclude, even if you cannot follow any of the above practices, due to various constraints and pressures in practical situations like (for example)

- The day a student is having his or her board exam (In anxiety)

- On the day an office goer is in the midst of facing a personal assessment and undergoing the related pressures at work front (under pressure)

- One is in the rush to catch an early morning flight (working under a time target).

please make it a habit to sit in one place for just two minutes. It does not matter whether you have taken bath or not, whether you have already eaten or not, whether you are wearing your shoe or not. Recite Gayatri mantra at least once with focussed mind. (As a Nitya Karma - a daily activity).

This will only help to tune your equipment "Mind" to face that day's situation most effectively.

The most important thing is to do it, do it, and do it.

▶▶▶▶

GLOSSARY		
Word	**Section No**	**Meaning**
Abivadhanam	6.9.4	Reverential salutation, respectful obeisance - including one's own name, title etc.
Achamanam	5.1	Sipping water - before religious ceremonies, before and after meals etc. - from the palm of the hand
Agni	7.1	Fire - there are three types of fires referred to as Garhapatya, Aghavaniya and Dakshina
Agnihotra	4.0	Maintenance of the sacred fire and offering oblations to it
Argya pradhanam	5.9	A respectful offering or oblation to god or a venerable person
Asmarohanam	2.2.D	Ascend or climb on a solid material - a stone or iron
Aswamedha yaga	4.1	A horse sacrifice
Atharva	5.0	One part of the Vedas

Word	Section No	Meaning
Atma parishechanam	5.8	Sprinkling over, moistening one self
Avahanam	6.6	Inviting or invoking a deity to be present
Bhakti	1.7.2	Devotion
Bhu, Bhuva, Suva, Maha, Jana.Tapa, sathya	5.3	The different planes (vyahrutis) in the cosmos. There are seven such planes (akin to modern frequency bands). They are also used as mystic syllables
Biksha	2.2.D	A means of subsistence - by asking, begging, soliciting Also means wages/living charges
Brahman	6.11	The supreme being
Brahmana, Kshatriya, Vaisya, Shudhra	3.3	The four classes/ sections in the society
Brahmo - padesam	2.1	Initiation to the holy mantra

Word	Section No	Meaning
Devata	6.5	A god, a portion/ characteristic of the supreme energy
Dhyana, Dhyanam	5.2	Meditation
Dig devata vandhan	6.9.5	Prostration to the gods in charge of various sides
Dvija	4.0	Twice born - refers to a person who has gone from one stage to another in life
Ganesh	5.2	A god - who protects from hurdles/blocks in carrying out an activity
Gayatri.Gayatri mantra	6.0	A sacred verse also refers to a vedic metre, Gayatri metre is a rhythm consisting of 24 syllables - arranged in as a triplet of eight syllables each
Gotra	2.2	Lineage
Guru	2.1	Teacher, preceptor, a respected person

Word	Section No	Meaning
Harihara	6.9.7	A particular form of deity consisting of Vishnu and Shiva conjoined
Ikyaaanu sandhana	5.11	Investigation of oneness or unity with the Supreme being
Japam	6.0	A muttered prayer, a constant repetition of a mantra
Karma	8.1	Performance of religiousrites
Karma anushtana	8.1	Practicing ones duties
Kashi yatra	3.3.8	Pilgrimage to Kashi, a celebrated city on the banks of Ganges (near modern Benaras)
Kumara bhojanam	2.2.D	Boys of similar age/ peers sit together to eat
Lokas	6.7	The world, division of Universe
Madhyanhika	5.6	Mid-day, belonging to noon

▶▶▶▶

Word	Section No	Meaning
Marjanam	5.5	Cleansing, purifying either by sprinkling oneself or by a third person with water by means of hand or a blade of Kusa grass etc.
Mitra	6.8	The sun
Namaskaram	6.0	Prostration
Nithya karma	10.0	Daily ritual/activity
Nyasa	6.7	Assignment of various parts of the body to several deities (energy forms) - mentally, also means location
Om	4.0	A sacred syllable of Hindus, an emblem of Supreme
Padmasana	6.0	A particular posture used in religious meditation
Palagai	6.0	A seat generally made out of wood
Parameshwara	5.4	Lord Shiva, the Supreme being

Word	Section No	Meaning
Parishechanam	8.0	Sprinkling over, moistening, Also means - in full or completely
Poonal/ yagya paveetham	2.2	Tamil word commonly used for the threads
Pradhakshinam	6.8	A reverential salutation - to go round from left to right
Pranava mantra	6.4	The sacred syllable Om
Pranayam	5.3,3.6	Restraining the breadth
Prasanam	5.6	Making one eat or taste
Pratha-sandhya	5.6	Morning Sandhya vandhanam
Pravara	2.2	A noble ancestor who has contributed to the credit of a Gotra or family
Prayaschiththa	5.9	Atonement
Raksha	6.11	Protection/preservation

▶▶▶▶

Word	Section No	Meaning
Rig	5.0	One part of Vedas
Rta	6.9.7	Order, truth, it also means water in some context
Sama	5.0	Sama veda, a metrical hymn
Samashti abhivandhan	6.9	Joint prayer
Samitadhanam	7.0	A prayer offering samith as the oblation
Sandhi	3.1	Union, peace, a joint
Sandhya	3.1	Twilight. Also means - meditation
Sandhya vandhanam	1.6	Prayer offered at time of sandhya
Sankalpam	5.4	Will, desire
Samarpanam	6.10	Delivering or handing over to
Samith/samidh	7.0	Fuel used for sacred fire
Samskara	7.0	Refinement, education, training

Word	Section No	Meaning
Saraswati	6.6	Goddess of learning
Sarpa	6.9.9	A snake
Satyam	6.9.7	Truth
Savita	6.6.7	originator of the Universe Refers to sun also
Savitri	6.6	A celestial verse of rig Veda, a celebrated verse of Rig Veda -so called as it is addressed to Sun, a ray of light, Goddess Parvati
Sayam Sandhya	5.6	Evening prayer - Sandhya Vandhanam
Shaaka	2.2	A branch, a part
Shraddha	5.0	Faith, respect
Shuddhi	5.5	Purification, correction
Soorya Narayana, Surya	6.8B	Sun
Sutra	2.2	A precept or aphorism Also means a thread

Word	Section No	Meaning
Swaha	5.6	An exclamation used in offering oblations to gods
Tharpanam	5.13	Presenting oblations of water
Upanayanam	2.1	Investiture with a sacred thread
Upanishads	2.0	A portion of the philosophical literature of Hindus
Upakarma	2.0	A ceremony performed before commencing to read the vedas -generally after the monsoon season
Upasthanam	6.8.	A Prayer
Upavitam	2.2	Sacred thread worn by Hindus over the left shoulder and goes under the right arm
Vandhanam	1.6	Obeisance
Varuna	6.8	A deity presiding over the sea

Word	Section No	Meaning
Ved Vyas	1.7.5	Holy saint who is regarded as the "arranger" of the Vedas in the present form
Veda pathashalas	1.7.5	School where they teach Hindu scriptures especially Vedas
Vedas	5.0	Sacred knowledge, the scripture of Hindus
Virinchi, Narayana, sankaratmane	6.9.8	The three characteristics of the supreme being - creation, protection and destruction - commonly referred to as Brahma, Vishnu and Shiva
Vyahrutis	4.0	Frequency bands, rhythms (the cosmos is created with the 7 rhythms)
Yagya	6.9.9	Sacrifice, a rite also means any oblation, offering
Yajur/yajus	5.0	A portion of Vedas used in sacrifices/a sacrificial prayer or formula

▶▶▶▶

Word	Section No	Meaning
Yama	6.9.6	God of death, also means - self control
Yoga,Yogi	3.6	A system of philosophy, joining/uniting with the Supreme

Printed in the United States
By Bookmasters